MURDERS & MY_____,
PEOPLE & PLOTS

A BUCKS, BEDS & NORTHANTS
MISCELLANY

by
John Houghton

Pictures
by
Norman Kent

ALL ROYALTIES TO
THE HOSPICE OF OUR LADY & ST. JOHN,
WILLEN

First published June 1993
by
The Book Castle
12 Church Street
Dunstable
Bedfordshire LU5 4RU

© John Houghton, 1993

The right of John Houghton to be identified as the Author of this
work has been asserted by him in accordance with the Copyright,
Designs and Patents Act, 1988.

ISBN 1 871199 76 X

Front Cover: Benjamin Keach uses the Pillory
                 as a Pulpit in Winslow in 1664.

Computer typeset by Keyword, Aldbury, Hertfordshire.
Printed by The Alden Press, Oxford

CONTENTS

PREFACE

My previous book, *Tales from Milton Keynes*, told of people and places, past and present, in and around the City. This present book uses the same formula, but the net is cast much wider.

Here are tales from the three counties of Buckinghamshire, Bedfordshire and Northamptonshire. The tales in both books are tales of fact, not fiction.

All the photographs in this book are the work of one man, Norman Kent, and were specially taken for this volume. I am indebted to him for his whole-hearted collaboration.

My thanks, too, to Fiona Smith, calligrapher, for her map and to Lord Campbell for his kind Foreword.

John Houghton

ABOUT THE AUTHOR

John Houghton was born in 1916 in Eastbourne. After graduating at Durham University he was ordained in 1939. He was Curate at Wolverton 1939–42. He served in Northern Rhodesia/Zambia from 1942 to 1973 and was awarded the Zambian Order of Distinguished Service in 1966. He is a Canon Emeritus of Lusaka Cathedral. From 1974 to 1983 he was National Promotions Secretary in Britain for Feed The Minds. He retired in 1983 and lives in Bletchley.

FOREWORD

by Lord Campbell of Eskan, former Chairman of
Milton Keynes Development Corporation

I am delighted to write a short Foreword to John Houghton's new
book: *Murders and Mysteries, People and Plots.*

His collection of stories covers the area where three counties
meet – Buckinghamshire, Bedfordshire and Northamptonshire. All
the towns and countless villages yield their rich harvest of
fascinating stories of people and events over the past three
centuries.

Milton Keynes is young – twenty-five in 1992. Yet a score of
places within its boundaries figured in the Domesday Book in
1086. Over the centuries, here and hereabouts, there have been
villains and heroes. The famous and the infamous have their
places, including those who planned the Gunpowder Plot of 1605
and the Great Train Robbery of 1963.

There have been eccentrics, like Browne Willis in the 18th
century, and Richard Carpenter in the 17th. Great literary figures
lived in these parts, among them poets like Cowper and Newton,
diarists like Cole, and moralists like Bunyan. Murderers too, and
their victims. And the 'fine lady who rode a white horse to
Banbury Cross' was Celia Fiennes, of Stowe and Broughton Castle,
in whose diary in the 1660s are descriptions of a dozen places in
this area as she saw them three hundred years ago.

All these and many other people, places and events are included
in this book. Here you can learn why a choirboy is stood on his head
in Leighton Buzzard every May; why oranges are rolled down
Dunstable Downs on Good Friday, and why oak-leaf garlands adorn
the monument of Charles II in Northampton once a year.

Willen was always a tiny village, but no part of Milton Keynes
has a more fascinating history. In the Willen story the Hospice of
Our Lady and St. John provides the climax of some eight hundred
years of Willen's history. *It is splendid to know that all the Royalties
on this book are to go to the Hospice.*

John Houghton's words and Norman Kent's admirable
photographs could hardly be devoted to a more worthy cause.

Lord Campbell of Eskan

LIST OF ILLUSTRATIONS

Barton
Seagrave

Brixworth

Ashby
St. Ledgers

Holdenby

Church
Brampton

NORTHAMPTON

DELAPRE ABBEY
ELEANOR CROSS

NORTHAMPTONSHIRE

Olney

Emberton

BEDFORD

Elstow

Gayhurst

Newport
Pagnell

Sulgrave

WHITTLEWOOD
FOREST

New Bradwell

Wolverton

Moulsoe

HOUGHTON
HOUSE

Deanshanger

Stony
Stratford

MILTON
KEYNES

Passenham

Calverton

STOWE
HOUSE

Beachampton

Aspley Guise

Ampthill

Thornborough

Bletchley

Fenny
Stratford

Woburn

WOBURN
ABBEY

Buckingham

Gawcott

Newton
Longville

BEDFORDSHIRE

Adstock

Gt. Horwood

Addington

Mursley

Winslow

Swanbourne

Soulbury

Hockliffe

Stewkley

Granborough

Linslade

Leighton
Buzzard

BUCKINGHAMSHIRE

Aston
Abbotts

Hardwick

Mentmore

Wingrave

DUNSTABLE

DUNSTABLE
DOWNS

Bierton

HERTFORDSHIRE

Brill

AYLESBURY

Lr. Winchendon

Dinton

Ford

Long
Crendon

Haddenham

Berkhamsted

CALLIGRAPHER : FIONA SMITH

vii

BIBLIOGRAPHY

Sheahan:	History & Topography of Buckinghamshire.
Gibbs, ed.:	The Buckinghamshire Miscellany.
Uttley:	Buckinghamshire.
Markham:	History of Milton Keynes and District.
J G Jenkins:	The Dragon of Whaddon.
John Camp:	Portrait of Buckinghamshire.
Lipscomb:	History & Antiquities of Buckinghamshire.
Harman:	Sketches of the Buckinghamshire Countryside.
John R Connon:	Elora.
Sir Edward Cook:	Life of Florence Nightingale (2 vols.).

Chapter 1

THEY LIVED HERE ONCE

All over London familiar blue plaques can be seen on the walls of houses. From them the passer-by can learn the names of famous people who once lived in those houses.

No such blue plaques adorn the walls of any houses in our towns and villages. Yet this area has been home, though sometimes only briefly, for an impressive number of famous people.

Olney will be for ever associated with the poet, William Cowper, and the converted slave-trader vicar, John Newton. Henry Gauntlett, 'the father of English Church music', and composer of an astonishing 10,000 hymn tunes, was also born and brought up in Olney.

Elstow and Bedford claim John Bunyan, author of Pilgrim's Progress, of which everybody knows, but also of about fifty other works, of which most folk are unaware.

Florence Nightingale's connection with Claydon House is well-known. The Florence Nightingale Room there is full of memorabilia of the 'Lady with the Lamp' of Crimean War fame. But it might all have been very different. Just how different you can read in Chapter 18 – 'Carrying the torch for the Lady with the Lamp'.

A tiny cottage, one room deep and about three rooms long, stands by the side of the Buckingham Road just after the turning to Great Horwood. It is nearly two hundred years old, and is known to many as Fay Compton's cottage – a tiny rural retreat to which she could escape after her West End successes.

The Registry Office in Fenny Stratford, scene of so many

*Fay Compton's
cottage on the
Buckingham
Road, a country
retreat after
west-end
successes.*

civil weddings nowadays, was once the town house of Sir John
French, the World War I General. Bracknell House was their
first married home after John French, then a young lieutenant,
had married Eleanora Anna, one of the eight daughters of
Richard Selby-Lowndes. John French subsequently rose to the
highest rank in the Army, and became a Field Marshall. He was
first knighted and then raised to the peerage as Lord French, 1st
Earl of Ypres. From 1918 to 1921 he was Viceroy of Ireland.
Later he retired to France where he died. But his widow, who
died in 1941, is buried in Bletchley Churchyard.

Bracknell House, Fenny Stratford's Registry Office. It was the first married home of Sir John French, World War I Field Marshall, and Viceroy of Ireland.

Wolverton House is where John Habgood, Archbishop of York since 1983, was born. His father was a much respected family doctor. And Bow Brickhill also had a famous resident – Sir Sydney Nicholson. (See page 107).

John Wilkes, that stormy petrel of 18th century politics, was once the owner of Eaton Leys Farm and Mill at Water Eaton. He took out a mortgage on the farm to help pay for his successful campaign to become MP for Aylesbury. But it was his later career, as Editor of the paper, The North Briton, that led him into such controversy. He was declared an outlaw and fled to France, returning later to face imprisonment. He went on to become Sheriff of Middlesex and Lord Mayor of London.

Sir Everard Digby, the owner of Gayhurst, became deeply involved in the Gunpowder Plot of 1605, and was hanged, drawn and quartered for that involvement. A gruesome tradition says that his executioner cut out his heart. He held it aloft for all to see, shouting 'Here is the head of a traitor!', whereupon Sir Everard Digby cried out: 'Thou art a liar!'

Catherine of Aragon was an involuntary resident in this area for some months. She was kept at Ampthill Manor while the annulment of her marriage to Henry VIII was being pushed through at meetings held at Dunstable Priory.

Two more of Henry VIII's six wives had local connections. Ann Boleyn's father, the Earl of Wiltshire, was Lord of the Manor of Aylesbury. And Ann herself, fated to be executed by Henry VIII, was known as 'the fair maid of Aylesbury' when Henry first courted her. Her successor, Henry's sixth and last wife, Catherine Parr, lived at Beachampton House.

The famous architect, Sir Gilbert Scott, was born in the Rectory at Gawcott, near Buckingham, in 1811. His father was the Vicar. His architectural record almost defies belief. He designed or restored thirty-eight cathedrals, nearly five hundred churches, and some two hundred secular buildings, including St. Pancras Station. The Albert Memorial is his work too. As Professor of Architecture at the Royal Academy he acquired a huge reputation with the brilliance of his lectures. He died in 1888 and is buried in Westminster Abbey, but his roots are pure Bucks.

Beecham's Little Liver Pills became a household name. Their creator lived at Mursley Hall. He had a reputation of eccentricity. However, his grandson brought more fame to the family name than even the famous Liver Pills. That grandson was Sir Thomas Beecham, the celebrated conductor.

The Abbots of St. Alban's Abbey in medieval times had a country retreat between Aylesbury and Leighton Buzzard, known still as Aston Abbots. After the dissolution of the monasteries in the 16th century the abbey buildings at Aston were reduced in size and survived as Aston House. Here in the 19th century lived Sir James Clark Ross, discoverer of the Magnetic North Pole. He later tried to reach the South Pole but was unsuccessful. Ross Island, and the Great Ross Ice Barrier in Antarctica are named after him. He lies buried in the churchyard at Aston Abbots.

In the 1950s Winslow had a renowned artist. He was Stuart Tresilian and he lived in Sheep Street. He was commissioned by Rudyard Kipling to illustrate the famous Jungle Books. Later, he also illustrated the book on the Antarctic Expedition of Sir Vivian Fuchs and Sir Edmund Hilary.

The village of Addington lies off the Winslow/Buckingham road. In 1924 the Reverend Gerard Olivier became Vicar there, just at the time that his teen-age son, Laurence Olivier, was about ready to go to Drama School in London. For several years he had been choirboy and acolyte in his father's churches and in other churches too. Those had been the first public performances of the future great theatrical knight.

Addington was home for a while to another famous person too. The celebrated composer and conductor, Sir Malcolm Sargent, lived in a cottage there in World War II, and occasionally helped out on the village church organ.

Paris House was built for the Paris Exhibition of 1878 and then re-erected in Woburn Abbey Park. The Queen Mother's brother and General de Gaulle have been among its occupants.

5

In Woburn Abbey Park stands Paris House. It is a building of Tudor style but it dates only from 1878. It is called Paris House for a very good reason – it was originally built in pre-fabricated sections for the Paris Exhibition of 1878. When that Exhibition closed the Duke of Bedford bought the house, had it dismantled, and re-erected in Woburn Park.

Paris House has had many uses, and many distinguished occupants. The much-loved Duchess Mary used it as part of the Hospital she created at Woburn. So for some time it was popularly known as 'The Tonsil Hospital'. At the beginning of the World War II the house was lived in by the Queen Mother's brother. King George VI and Queen Elizabeth spent many weekends there during the war years. General de Gaulle also lived in the house for some time. In more recent times it became a Restaurant.

But Northamptonshire boasts a home of far greater historical importance. A Lancashire man named Lawrence Washington moved to Northamptonshire in about 1530. He prospered as a wool merchant. In 1532, and again in 1545, he was Mayor of Northampton. His ambition was to build himself a country seat. This he achieved by building Sulgrave Manor in the Northamptonshire countryside in about 1560. The family continued to live in the house.

In the 17th century they were Royalist in sympathy. In the Civil War one member of the family, the Reverend Lawrence Washington, was ejected from his parish by the Parliamentarians. When the Civil War was over, and Cromwell was Protector, another member of the family, John Washington, son of the ejected priest, emigrated to Virginia in 1656. In America John Washington's family prospered. His great-grandson, born in February 1732, was General George Washington, the first President of the United Stated of America.

Chapter 2

MURDER MOST FOUL

On the evening of December 29th, 1170, Thomas à Becket, the Archbishop of Canterbury, was murdered in his own Cathedral by four Knights who thought they were doing what the King wanted. The murder shocked the country and Thomas was regarded as a martyr. Soon pilgrims were flocking to his shrine.

The murder of Archbishop Thomas à Becket in 1170 was depicted on murals in Winslow Church in the 15th century.

Three centuries later, in the 15th century, in the Parish Church of St. Lawrence in Winslow, large murals were painted on the walls of the nave. One of them depicted that murder in Canterbury Cathedral. Remains of the murals can still be seen today, though by now they are hardly decipherable.

In Swanborne in the 17th century there was a family by the name of Adams. They were good honest yeoman stock, pillars of society, and devout worshippers at their parish church. Head of the family was Thomas Adams who became a good solid citizen and Freeman of the City of London. He lived happily with his wife, Elizabeth, who had borne him four children. Their names were Robert, Thomas, Alice and Johan.

All in all, then, a happy and prosperous family, whose happiness was shattered on the day when Thomas Adams left Swanborne to go into Leighton Buzzard on business. He never returned. He was mugged and left for dead. So his wife was widowed and his children left fatherless.

A brass in the floor of the chancel of Swanborne Church records the sad tale:

> 'Here lyeth buried ye bodie of Thomas Adams
> of this parish yeoman & Freeman of London
> whoe had to wife Elizabeth and by her 4 children
> viz. Robert, Thomas, Alice and Johan.'

> 'Hee departed this life ye 17 of October, 1626.'

There follows this sad verse which tells what happened:

> 'Behold in him the fickle state of man
> which holie David likened to a span
> In prime of youth by bloudie thieves was slaine
> in Liscombe Ground his blood ye grasse did staine.
> O cruel death – yet God turns all to best
> for out of misery hee has gone to rest.'

A Swanborne worthy mugged in 1626 and left for dead.

How Noble Eddens Died

Not so far from Swanborne, in Thame Churchyard, lies another murder victim, Noble Eddens. Like Adams, he was a worthy, hard-working citizen – not as well-born as Adams, but well respected. His name wasn't really Noble – that was just a nickname reflecting his sturdy upright frame.

He lived in Thame and worked as a market Gardener in Crendon. His field was on high ground and gave him a good view of the surrounding countryside. One day in 1828 he looked up from his work and in the distance saw two men acting suspiciously. He watched as they detached a sheep from the flock and killed it. He recognised them as two ne'er-do-wells from Thame.

He could have denounced them, but didn't do so. He knew that if they were tried and found guilty they would have been transported for life to Australia, or even hanged.

Long Crendon Court House. 'Noble' Eddens, murdered in 1828, had a nearby Nursery Garden.

But even if he didn't inform on them, he wanted to let them know that he knew of their crime. So, every time he met them, either on the road, or at market, or at the Inn, he would simply say: Baa!, Baa!, Baa!

They got the message. They knew that he knew, and they were determined to shut him up. Their chance came one Saturday night. Noble Edden had been to Aylesbury Market. As he drove home in his cart he picked up a Haddenham man and gave him a lift. As they went along Noble told his passenger that he had an uneasy feeling that something bad was about to happen. The passenger offered to stay with him instead of alighting near his home, but Noble said there was no need. So the passenger alighted and Noble continued alone in his cart. Very soon after that the attack came. It was violent and noisy and was overheard by people some distance away.

Meanwhile, at that very moment, in Noble Edden's home in Thame, his wife was busy ironing in her kitchen. Suddenly she stopped, screamed, and put down her iron. 'Oh dear God, my husband is being murdered!' Her neighbours rushed in to her in alarm and she told them she had 'seen' her husband being assaulted with a hammer by a man called Tyler. Lanterns were fetched and Mrs Edden and her neighbours set out to look for Noble.

The badly battered body of Noble Edden was found in the Haddenham field. The horse and cart were found later in another field. Noble's body was taken to the Cider House where, next day, the Inquest was held. The only verdict possible at that time was: 'Murder by some persons unknown'. The body was released for burial.

But before the burial took place Mrs Edden loudly demanded that Tyler be brought and made to touch the body. She was convinced that he was the culprit, just as she had seen in her vision. If he was forced to touch the body, some sign would surely manifest itself. Despite her repeated demands Tyler refused to come anywhere near the body.

The burial took place and weeks passed. Many in Thame were convinced that Tyler, and another man called Sewell, were the murderers, but in the absence of proof or witnesses nothing could be done.

Noble Edden's son took over his murdered father's business, and made the same round of the markets as his father had done. Late one night, riding back to Thame, two men leapt out of a hedge and tried to board his cart. Young Edden whipped up his horse, and lashed out also at his attackers. One of them called out: 'We'll serve you the same as we served your father!' Young Edden recognised them both – Tyler and Sewell.

Spring changed to summer in the following year, and in August Sewell was arrested and taken to Aylesbury. While in custody he said that Tyler (who had left Thame) was the one who had killed Noble Edden with a stone-mason's hammer. Tyler, located up-country, was arrested and brought back to Thame. When the case was tried Sewell's evidence was not accepted and Tyler was discharged. Sewell, too, was released, but was immediately re-arrested on a charge of chicken-stealing. He was found guilty and sentenced to fourteen years' transportation. Desperate to get this harsh sentence reduced, Sewell again accused Tyler of Edden's murder, and this time he was believed. Tyler was again arrested and both of them were put on trial. They were found guilty, and were hanged outside Aylesbury Gaol.

The Issue of the Bucks. Record for March 8th, 1830 carried this report:

Some 4000 or 5000 people assembled this morning in front of Aylesbury Gaol to witness the execution of Tyler and Sewell. Those who are fond of such sights must have been satisfied with the rich treat it afforded them; it was a regular old-fashioned hanging match. There seemed to be an absence of solemnity about the whole matter and it was hard to understand that what was going on was a reality. The poor wretches looked more like puppets in the hands of a showman than men on the very verge of death – it appeared like a stage play altogether.

Sewell first made an appearance and he continued that silly half-idiotic conduct he had maintained all through the business, which, whether assumed or real, could only be known to those well acquainted with his antecedents. He looked searchingly among the crowd, anxious to see anyone he knew, and seemed disappointed he saw so few. He recognised a Mr Taylor and shouted out: "Ahh, Mr Taylor, there you are! I am just going to die and I hope I shall go to Heaven; so goodbye, Mr Taylor, goodbye".

Tyler was then brought out and he was very nervous and trembling. He advanced to the front and spoke to the following effect: "My blessed brothers, I wish to say a few words to you before I quit this world, which will be in a few moments; and I hope you will all take warning by my untimely fate, though I am innocent of the act for which I am about to suffer. I am just going to leave this world, and I do solemnly declare that my life has been taken away by false swearers. I bear them no malice, but freely forgive them, and I hope God will bless you all".

Here the poor wretch's speech failed him; he appeared to have had something more to say, but was prevented by the interference of the executioner who pulled a cap over his eyes. In another minute both criminals were launched into eternity.'

Betrayed by his Own Dog

Another public execution which proved a crowd-puller was that of a ratcatcher-cum-chimney sweeper named Corbet. He was hanged in front of a vast crowd of spectators at Bierton in July 1773. He had broken into a house, accompanied by his dog, and had murdered the householder, Richard Holt. Unfortunately for him, when he fled from the house, he inadvertently left his dog behind inside! All the authorities had to do was to release the dog and follow it. It made its way unerringly to its master who was found in possession of goods, stolen from Mr Holt, found guilty and sentenced to be hanged.

The hanging on that July day in 1773 took place at Gib Lane between Bierton and Hulcott. It had a grisly post-script – the body was not taken down from the gibbet for twenty years! It hung there, at the top of the eighteen foot gibbet, wrapped round by iron bands, from 1773 to 1795. In 1774 a passing 'humourist' offered half-a-crown to anyone who would climb the gibbet and adorn the murderer's remains with a black scarf and pair of gloves. A local shepherd accepted the challenge and claimed the half-crown. Soon only the skull remained of the late and unlamented Corbet. When the gibbet itself was finally taken down part of it was used as a gatepost. But from the rest of the timber an enterprising Mr Watts made and sold carved souvenirs.

Murdered by the Butcher

A century before the despatch of Corbet on the gibbet at Bierton, another murderer met the same fate on the gibbet at Calverton. He was a Stony Stratford butcher and his hanging took place in 1694. His victim, said to have been his cousin, was not a popular lady. She was the wealthy widow of the Lord of the Manor, Simon Bennet. She seems to have lived in a perpetual state of feud with her neighbours and tenants, and she conducted a running dispute with the Rector over the payment of tithes.

It was common knowledge that she kept lots of money in the Manor House and it was perhaps inevitable that some one, some day, would break in and try to steal it. Cole, in his Blechely Diary, records: '. . . being of a miserable disposition, she lived by herself in the old house at Calverton; and being supposed to have great store of money by her, a butcher of Stony Stratford artfully got into the house, and there being nobody to assist her, or call for help, he barbarously murdered her circa 1691, for which he was afterwards executed.'

It happened on the night of Stony Stratford's Horse and Hiring Fair. The butcher was an immediate suspect. He was arrested, tried, and condemed. He was hanged on the gibbet in Gib Lane, Calverton, in 1694. Local tradition says that the lady was killed in the servants' hall. A stone in the farmhouse wall still marks the spot near where the gibbet used to stand. Faintly carved on the stone is the outline of two gibbets, and the date is 1693. Some say this date refers to the unpopular Grace Bennet's murder, not to the murderer's hanging, which took place a year later.

Graffiti on a Calverton farm wall records a nasty murder in 1693.

Death in Newton Longville . . .

No hanging, public or otherwise, followed a nastly little murder in March 1814 in Newton Longville. The victim was a well-known, longtime resident in the village. He was Mr Verney and he kept a chandler's shop. Nobody knows at what time he was murdered. He was simply found early one evening in his shop, very severely wounded in the head and various other parts of his body. It seemed clear from his wounds that he had been viciously assaulted with a mallet or a hammer. But why? And by whom?

15

He was still alive when they found him – just – but he was too far gone to be able to give any account of what had happened. Twenty minutes after he was found in that parlous state, he was dead.

The strangest feature of the case was that though Mr Verney had been so severely wounded, nothing was stolen either from his person or his shop.

... And at Hanslope

In July 1912 Edward Watts, Lord of the Manor, was shot at Hanslope Park by his own head gamekeeper, William Farrow. Edward Watts and his wife were walking home after attending church on that Sunday morning in July. The gamekeeper had a grievance – he was under notice of dismissal. He was also drunk, having taken too much homemade wine on an empty stomach. Having twice shot Edward Watts fatally, and narrowly missing Mrs Watts, gamekeeper Farrow ran into the nearby woods and shot himself.

The widow caused some eyebrows to be raised, when after her husband was buried, she arranged for a headstone to be erected over his grave bearing the cryptic inscription:

'Waiting till all shall be revealed'.

Chapter 3

A HARVEST OF FESTIVALS

There is no festival more widespread or more popular than the Harvest Festival. It happens each year in churches and chapels large and small, in town and in country. But there are many other festivals too, and many other customs and observances, some of them very local and many of them quaint. A whole harvest of festivals in fact. And some of them are peculiar to our three counties.

But let us look at Harvest Festivals first. Some people say it was a village parson in Cornwall who 'invented' the Harvest Festival last century. There is some confusion about who this parson was. Some say it was Parson Hawkes, while others say it was a Vicar called Kingdom. Either way, the most that can be said for Parson Hawkes (or was it Parson Kingdom?) is that he designed the particular pattern or style of Harvest Festivals as we have come to know them.

No Harvest Festival would be complete without the singing of the hymn, *'We plough the fields and scatter the good seed on the land'*. The occasion, and that hymn, somehow typify a very British institution. British? Not quite. That hymn dates from the 18th century, and was written in Germany by a German Agricultural Commissioner, and he wrote it for a Harvest Festival *he* devised about a hundred years before Hawkes (or Kingdom?) And if we go back another hundred years before that, to the beginning of the 17th century, we find John Donne, Dean of St. Paul's Cathedral, preaching a very fine Harvest Festival sermon more than three hundred and fifty years ago. Here is part of what he said in that sermon:

*'God made sun and moon to distinguish seasons, and day
and night, and we cannot have the fruits of the earth but
in their seasons. But God has made no decree to
distinguish the seasons of His mercies. In Paradise the
fruits were ripe in the first minute, and in heaven it is
always autumn – His mercies are ever in their maturity.
We ask for our daily bread, and God never says: You
should have come yesterday – He never says: You must
come again tomorrow, but: " Today if you will hear His
voice, Today He will hear you "'*

But if we really want to get to the true origins of Harvest
Festivals we must go much further back than to Hawkes or
Kingdom last century, or to the German Agriculturist two
hundred years ago, or to John Donne at St. Paul's Cathedral
three hundred and fifty years ago. We must go back four
thousand years to the time of Moses. It's all there in
Deuteronomy, chapter 26, where the people were told to bring
the first-fruits of the harvest into the Temple, and there they
were to do four things: to remember, to give thanks, to worship,
and to share. And centuries later these same four ingredients
still mark a Harvest Festival.

Apart from the Harvest Festival in church or chapel, there
used to be other traditional observances also. Sixty years ago a
retired North Bucks. teacher wrote a delightful book: 'Sketches
of the Bucks. Countryside'. He talked to the old men and wrote
down what he learned from them:

*'For many years each farmer celebrated the "Harvest
Home" by a supper to his men and their wives in his
barn . . . but the old custom was allowed to lapse.
However, the cottagers for some time after celebrated the
ingathering of the harvest by the "Largess" which was
the gift of an eighteen-gallon cask of beer from the
brewery. It was delivered by a drayman wearing a
red-tasseled cap. On an appointed evening the villagers
met . . . those requiring it bringing their own bread and
cheese. After the homely repast was finished, songs were
called for, and the meeting became quite convivial.'*

*Why is a
Leighton
Buzzard
choirboy stood
on his head on
a Monday
morning in
May? (Or it
could be a
choirgirl.)*

About four months before Harvest celebrations in September and October, there is another annual observance in May called Rogationtide. Rogation means 'asking'. Traditionally, blessing is asked in the spring on the crops for whose harvesting thanks will be offered in the autumn. This ancient custom was started in the 4th century in France by Bishop Mamertus. There had been an earthquake and the result was likely to be poor crops and starvation. The good Bishop urged the people to make processions round all their parishes and to offer litanies. So began the custom of 'beating the bounds', followed locally each year in several places. Waddeston, for example, established a tradition for 'beating the bounds' every seven years round the combined parishes of

Waddeston, Westcott and Wrodham. It took two days to complete the perambulation. 'The Bounders' followed the old Rogationtide tradition of marking the boundaries and spanking young boys over the boundary stones 'to impress the place upon them'.

But Leighton Buzzard has its own very special observance of the custom. It takes place of Rogation Monday in May. But it is not itself a Rogationtide custom. Instead, it commemorates the generosity of the man who founded Wilkes Almshouses in the town. A procession of Clergy and choirboys accompanies the Trustees of the Wilkes Charity along the High Street to Wilkes Almshouse. Arrived there, they sing a hymn, a prayer is said, and the Clerk reads an extract from the 17th century Will of Edward Wilkes, *while a choirboy stands on his head!* Nowadays, though, it is just as likely to be a choirgirl. In 1992 the honour fell to Jenny Wallace. Nobody quite knows the reasons for the peculiar custom. Nowadays a cushion is provided for the upturned chorister.

Simon and Nelly

Leighton Buzzard Parish Church has a famous piece of medieval graffiti which is said to illustrate the origin of Simnel Cake. This rich form of cake is traditionally eaten on Mothering or Mid-Lent Sunday. Laurence Whistler, in his book, 'The English Festivals', testifies to the widespread popularity of Simnel Cakes, and describes some of them: *'The Shrewsbury kind has a thick crust; the Devizes kind is in the shape of a star, crustless; the Bury kind is flattish, but thicker in the centre, compounded of currants and candied peel and generally round in shape and elongated'*. Whistler doesn't mention a Bucks. variety. The two figures in the Leighton Buzzard graffiti ('Simon and Nelly') are said to have quarrelled about how best to cook a cake to take home to mother on Mothering Sunday. Simon said it should be boiled, but Nelly said it should be baked. They compromised, first boiling it and then baking it. And that, they say, is the true origin of Simnel Cake!

Graffiti in Leighton Buzzard Church. 'Simon and Nelly' couldn't agree on how to make a Simnel Cake.

Blessing the Simnel Cake and Mothering Day posies at St. Martin's Church, Fenny Stratford.

Pancakes

Shrove Tuesday is an annual date rich in local custom. It is the day before Lent begins on Ash Wednesday and is popularly marked by the making and eating of pancakes. In Toddington when the 'Pancake Bell' is rung at St. George's Church, children make their way to Conger Hill. There they lie on the ground and listen for the bubbling of the witch's cauldron and the frying of her pancakes. Markyate and Wilstead also have Pancake Races.

Since 1445 Olney has had its own very special Shrove Tuesday Pancake Race. It is run from the Market Place to Church Lane, a distance of 415 yards. Warning bells are rung from the church steeple and then, at precisely 11.55, the Churchwarden rings the special bronze 'Pancake Bell' and the race is on. Only women of eighteen years and over may compete and they must be residents of Olney. They must wear a skirt, apron and headscarf, and carry a frying pan containing

It started in 1445, and it still goes on every Shrove Tuesday in Olney.

22

a pancake. The pancake must be tossed at the start of the race and again at the Finish. The winner is greeted by the Vicar with the Kiss of Peace, and is also kissed by the Churchwarden. After the race everyone, the runners, officials, townsfolk and visitors, crowd into the church for the great Shriving Service. There the competitors occupy seats reserved for them in the Chancel.

Olney v Kansas

In 1950 this unique race went 'international' because a challenge was received from the town of Liberal in Kansas, USA. Ever since then the two towns have competed annually and prizes are exchanged. The race in both places is timed and the winner is declared after the times are exchanged by a transatlantic telephone call. Up to 1992 the score between Olney and Liberal stood at twenty-one each, with one race void. The 1992 winner in Olney, Susan Jones, covered the 415 yards in 62.5 seconds, but Vicky Van Sickle in Liberal achieved a time of 61.5 seconds.

Here is how an old Ballad described the Olney Pancake Race in the days of the first Elizabeth:

> At Olney when good Bess was queen
> The pancake bell was rung,
> And sweeter sound ne'er scurried
> From steeple, crowde or tongue.
>
> The girls when Robin touched the rope
> Their batter made, and by it
> They stood, and at the first 'Ting Tang'
> Began straightway to fry it.
>
> The sizzling done, the sugar last
> They spread – sagacious people! –
> Then rushed with pan and pancake hot
> Pell-mell towards the steeple.

Ran one-and-twenty maids that morn,
As documents discover,
But Ann was far the fleetest for
The ringer was her lover.

He met her at the steeple step,
Said she, 'Not one has caught me'
Said he, and took his bite, 'By Schorne,
A better ne'er was brought me'.

Northampton Honours Charles II

Northampton has an unusual ceremony each year on May 29th. Oakapple wreaths are carried from the Town Hall into All Saints Church and at noon are placed on the statue of Charles II. Later in the day there is a service at which a Charity Sermon is preached. This ceremony does more than commemorate the escape of Charles II when he hid in an oak tree. It dates from 1675 and is an annual commemoration of the disastrous fire of that year, when much of the town was destroyed. King Charles II immediately gave Northampton a thousand tons of timber from Whittlewood Forest to build new houses. He also ordered that the town should be exempt from the paying of Chimney Tax for seven years. So Oak Apple Day in Northampton each May 29th is an expression both of gratitude and loyalty.

A number of places in northern England have traditional 'egg-pacing' ceremonies on Good Friday, symbolising the rolling away of the stone from Christ's tomb at the resurrection. Dunstable has its own version of the same custom. In Dunstable it is oranges, not eggs, that are rolled over Dunstable Downs for the children to scramble for.

Michaelmas, on September 29th, was often the occasion for special feasts and events. Stewkley was no exception, though the annual Stewkley Feast, originally held at Michaelmas, came to be celebrated on October 11th. On that day all landowners collected their rents and would then give a feast to their tenants, with roast beef and Christmas pudding. A travelling fair would arrive, and children were given two days' holiday to enjoy the feast.

Trinity Sunday once had its own customs in some places. Harman's 'Sketches of the Bucks. Countryside' related two such local annual feasts that are no more. One, which lasted till World War I, was at Twyford, near Steeple Claydon in Buckinghamshire. Asking an old-timer whether the Feast was still held, he was told:

> *No, that was done away with during the war. We had some fine times then. We were up by four in the morning and started decorating the front of the school where the dinner was held with boughs we had cut from the trees. At eleven O'clock everybody assembled and marched to church headed by the band. After service we marched back to the school again for dinner, then we enjoyed ourselves for the rest of the day. It was such a pity it was done away with, as everyone who had left the village returned on that day to meet his relations and his old friends. It was the day for family gatherings, but now it's gone, and I don't suppose it will ever come back again.'*

The same old-timer went on to tell of another such feast that used to be held at Godington. It was a very small place, he said, but it used to be crowded when the feast took place. Trinity Sunday was the date on which it was held. There was no Public House in those days, so one of the cottagers got a licence just for the week. He decorated the front of his cottage with boughs and for that reason it was called the Bough House. The cottager used to fetch a cart-load of ale, but that did not last long, for the house was kept open all day. And the old-timer continued:

> *'What used to attract so many was the fighting that took place. The best men from Tingewick, Gawcott, Twyford, Steeple Claydon, Fringford and other places for miles round, used to go to try their hand. And all the*

25

*challenges that had been made for months before used to
be settled on the green. If anybody had a quarrel with
another man in any village round about, one of them
would say, "I'll meet you at Godington Feast". It was the
recognised time for settling old scores, and it was a case
of bare fists every time. The Feast has been done away
with for some time now, and perhaps it's a good thing
too. It would never be allowed in these days.'*

Kat Stitch

Buckinghamshire used to be famous for lace-making. It was
both an art and an industry and its origins date back a long
way. In the 16th century Flemish weavers and lace-makers fled
to England. Some of them settled at Olney and Newport
Pagnell. Hanslope and Stony Stratford also became prominent
in Bone-lace. It was called Bone-lace because the bobbins were
made of bone.

*Lace Making bobbins. Did Catherine of Aragon introduce lace making to
North Bucks.?*

One tradition says that lace-making in North Bucks. started with Catherine of Aragon – Henry VIII's first wife. She had been given the Manor of Steeple Claydon by her royal husband. From those days right up to Victorian times, there was an annual festival for lace-makers at Claydon on what was called St. Katern's Day. One of the stitches in lace-making is called a 'Kat Stitch'.

Christingle

All over the country, there is nowadays a 'new' annual festival which is growing in popularity. It usually happens just before Christmas. Though a 'new' festival, it has ancient roots. The Romans in pre-Christian times had their own version of it; the ancient Welsh Church knew it too by the name 'Calenig'; and it was a feature of the ancient Moravian Church. It is called *Christingle*, which means 'Christ Light'.

Christingles – full of symbolism.

A Christingle is an orange into which a candle is inserted. Round the orange a red ribbon is fastened. Stuck into the orange are four cocktail sticks laden with nuts, raisins and sultanas. The whole assembly is rich in symbolism:

The orange represents the world created by God;
The candle represents Christ, the Light of the world;
The red ribbon represents His blood;
The four sticks represent the four seasons of the year;
The fruit represents the fruits of the earth;

And the whole *Christingle* represents God's love for His people.

A Christingle Nativity Play at Water Eaton, Christmas, 1991.

At a Christingle Service, just before Christmas, children come to church bringing gifts of money which they have collected for the work of the Children's Society. In a service of carols, readings and prayers they present their gifts and each in turn receives a Christingle.

The Children's Society, which exists to help children and families throughout England and Wales, introduced the Christingle Service in 1968. It is now an established feature every December in many places. So a new tradition has been born.

Individual Saints' Days are another rich source of local annual customs. Two example are provided by Olney and Fenny Stratford. Olney Parish Church is dedicated to St. Peter and St. Paul, with its annual patronal festival on June 29th. In the year 1316 a licence was granted to Ralf, Lord Bassett, for the holding of an annual fair. It was to be called The Cherry Fair. As well as being a church-related event, it was also in origin a commercial affair, for the selling of the cherries from the extensive orchards of those days. The licence specified that the fair should take place 'on the vigil, feast and morrow of St. Peter and St. Paul'. Its present-day successor is the annual Church Fete, still called The Cherry Fair. Cherries are still featured in it, though they are no longer the product of Olney Orchards.

Fenny Poppers
Fenny Stratford's parish church is St. Martin's, whose feast day is November 11th. When Browne Willis, the Lord of the Manor in the 18th century, built the church on the site of a former Chantry Chapel, he decreed that the Feast of St. Martin should be marked each year by the holding of a special service in church, and by a dinner, and by the firing three times during the day of the 'Fenny Poppers'. The Poppers, six in number, are cast-iron, made in the shape and size of beer tankards. They are stuffed with newspapers, primed with gunpowder, and ignited by a long rod heated in a brazier. They are fired at 12 noon, 2pm and 4pm. The custom is still observed annually, more than 260 years after Browne Willis first decreed it.

Finally, there is the touching little ceremony annually in Aylesbury Parish Church. There, by long custom, the Vicar on one day each year lays a fresh red flower on the tomb of the Lee family.

Each year, then, a whole Harvest of Festivals marks the passing of the months. It will be a sad day if, like the old feasts at Twyford and Godington, or St. Katern's Day at Claydon, any of them cease to be observed.

Chapter 4

RITES OF PASSAGE

These are what happen at crucial moments in the life of every individual. Most of all they concern birth, marriage, and death. Or, as it is sometime flippantly put, hatch, match, and despatch.

When the individuals to whom they happen are national figures – kings and queens especially, they have effects on everyone else. Our local history has certainly been affected by the rites of passage of our national leaders.

An early example is the death of William the Conqueror. When William defeated Harold at Hastings in 1066 he extended his control over the whole country by awarding Lordships and Manors to those who had supported his invasion. Some of these were his own kinsmen; some were knights who had contributed forces; and some were religious leaders. One such religious leader was Geoffrey, Bishop of Coutance in France. To him were awarded the Manors of Water Eaton, Bletchley, Fenny Stratford and Simpson.

When William I died in 1072 he was succeeded by his son, William Rufus who became William II. But William Rufus was not the eldest son of the Conqueror. The eldest son was Robert, Duke of Normandy, and a rebellion broke out in his favour. Geoffrey, Bishop of Coutance and Lord of the Manors of Water Eaton, Bletchley, Fenny Stratford and Simpson, was among those who supported Robert. The plot failed and the rebellion was put down. Bishop Geoffrey was made to pay for backing the losing side. In 1092 he was stripped of all his Manors in these parts and they were awarded instead to Walter Giffard, the first Earl of Buckingham. As a result the Giffard family

Queen Eleanor's Cross in Stony Stratford in the 13th century was destroyed in the Civil War in the 17th century. But it is not forgotten.

controlled North Bucks. for nearly a century.

Let's take next the moving story of Queen Eleanor – a story which has all three elements of hatch, match and despatch. The match came in 1254 when a marriage was arranged at Burgos in Spain between the ten year old daughter of King Ferdinand of Castille, Princess Eleanor, and the young English Prince Edward, the future King Edward I. In due time they married and the match proved a great success. And the match was very amply followed by hatch, for Queen Eleanor bore no less than fifteen children, four boys and eleven girls.

In 1290 the much-loved Queen Eleanor died, just outside Lincoln on a Royal Progress to Scotland. King Edward was heart-broken and decreed that his wife's body should be carried to London for burial in Westminster Abbey. At each place where her body rested on the twelve day funeral procession to London a stone cross would be erected in her memory. Among other places, the Queen's body rested overnight at Northampton, Stony Stratford, Woburn, Dunstable and St. Albans. At each place an Eleanor Cross was erected. The Northampton Cross survives to this day, but the Crosses at Stony Stratford, Woburn, Dunstable and St. Albans were all destroyed in the Civil War in the 17th century. But Stony Stratford today has a Queen Eleanor Street commemorating part of the route her cortege took. When she was finally buried in Westminster Abbey Thomas, a Master Craftsman from Leighton Buzzard fashioned the ironwork for her tomb. Leighton Buzzard church has a fine example of his workmanship on its west door.

We come now to the Wars of the Roses (1453–1485). There was plenty of 'hatch, match and despatch' then, much of which affected North Bucks. because of the involvement of the de Grey family, of the Manors of Wilton and Bletchley.

Henry VI towards the end of his reign was considered no longer able to rule his kingdom. So Richard, Duke of York, was appointed as Protector. Both he and several others believed that they had legitimate claims to the throne. In the rivalries and ambitions that emerged the great barons exerted their influence too.

The crown eventually. passed to Edward IV. As a handsome young King he came often to North Buckinghamshire and South Northamptonshire to hunt. On one such visit to Stony Stratford his hunting took him into Whittlewood Forest. There he met and fell in love with Elizabeth Woodville, the young widow of a member of the de Grey family.

The King married her, at first secretly, in 1464. Later their marriage was solemnised more formally. Elizabeth bore him two children, first Edward and then Richard. When these two sons were thirteen and eleven years respectively their father the king died in 1483. The young princes were then staying in Ludlow. The elder boy was proclaimed king and it was arranged that he and his younger brother should be accompanied to London. The date for the coronation was to be May 4th. When they reached Stony Stratford they were lodged in the High Street. It was here that their uncle, Richard, Duke of Gloucester, caught up with them and took control of their onward journey to London. He seemed to be caring affectionately for his young nephews, but when London was reached everything changed. An Assembly of Lords and Commons deposed the young Edward V before he could be crowned, alleging his illegitimacy. Richard, Duke of Gloucester was declared king instead and became Richard III.

When the two little Princes slept in Stony Stratford they didn't know they were on their way to be murdered in the Tower.

Who Murdered the Little Princes?

A wholesale slaughter accompanied this turn of events. Earl Rivers, the father of Elizabeth Woodville and therefore the maternal grandfather of the two young princes was murdered. So were two of his sons, Elizabeth's brothers. Lord Lionel Grey was murdered also. And, most heinous of all, so were the two little princes in the Tower.

All this was said to have been the work of the ambitious Richard, so that he might take the throne for himself. So Richard passed into history as the wicked uncle who murdered the two little royal princes who not so long before had slept peacefully in their beds in Stony Stratford High Street.

But was Richard the monster he was alleged to have been? The Tudor historian, Sir Thomas More, said that he was. So did Shakespeare. But others have said that it was all Tudor propaganda. To this day there are those who believe passionately that Richard was maligned and they continue in their efforts to rehabilitate his memory.

Next we come to Tudor times and to King Henry VIII. Plenty of 'hatch, match and despatch' in *his* story. Henry first married Catherine of Aragon. That was not Catherine's first marriage. She had previously been the wife of Henry VIII's older brother, Arthur the Prince of Wales. In that dynastic match King Henry VII had settled on his new daughter-in-law rents from lands in Buckinghamshire, at Steeple Claydon, Wendover, Wraysbury and Bierton. Catherine's husband died not long afterwards. Henry VII then successfully petitioned the Pope to allow the widowed Catherine of Aragon to be married to his second son, who later became Henry VIII.

That was the first of Henry's six matches. Unfortunately the matches were not followed by the right sort of hatches, for five of his six wives failed to produce sons. Despatch for two of them was cruel – Henry had them executed. The well-known catalogue neatly sums up what happened to all six: 'Divorced, beheaded, died; Divorced, beheaded, died'.

At Dunstable Priory a discussion was held leading to the decision that Henry's marriage to Catherine of Aragon could be annulled and so free him to marry Anne Boleyn. The motive was that Catherine had failed to bear Henry a son; the excuse was that Henry ought never to have married the widow of own brother.

In Henry's sixth and last match, his marriage to Catherine Parr, there is a real local connection, for Catherine Parr was related to several Bucks. families, and she lived at Beachampton House.

'The King is but a Knave'

The nation must have looked on in astonishment at the ever-changing kaleidoscope of King Henry VIII's matrimonial affairs. George Taylor of Newport Pagnell was charged in 1535 at Little Brickhill Assizes for having been heard to say: 'The king is but a knave and liveth in adultery and is an heretic and liveth not after the laws of God. I set not by the king's crown, and if I had it here I would play football with it'. Poor George defended himself as best he could. His first line of defence was that he never said it. And his second line of defence was that if he said it, he was drunk at the time. Neither line of defence did him much good. It was recommended that he should be hanged, drawn and quartered. (The Buckinghamshire Assizes were held regularly at Little Brickhill from 1433 and 1638. This was because it was the first accessible place for Judges coming from London on their 'Norfolk' Circuit.)

In 1547 Henry VIII died. In six matches he had hatched one son, a sickly child whose mother, Jane Seymour, died ten days later. Her son was not expected to live long either, but he survived to his early 'teens and was proclaimed King Edward VI. He had two half-sisters: Mary, the daughter of Catherine of Aragon, and Elizabeth, the daughter of Ann Boleyn. If the boy king died, either of them might succeed him. But both had been declared bastards following the divorces of their respective mothers.

A Nine Days' Wonder

There was one other possibility – Lady Jane Grey. She was a granddaughter of Henry VII, an intelligent and beautiful girl of sixteen. So a plot was hatched to make her queen when the young King Edward VI died. The Grey family of North Bucks. was naturally all in favour of such a move. Baron Grey, of Water Hall, Bletchley, had a son, Arthur, who was betrothed to Lady Jane Grey's sister, the eight year old Lady Mary. So there was enthusiasm for the plan to put Lady Jane Grey on the throne.

The young king died on July 6th 1553. Lady Jane Grey,

much against her will, was at once proclaimed Queen in London. But her proclamation was at once challenged by the supporters of Mary Tudor who gathered their forces on her behalf. In Bucks. Sir William Dormer of Wing proclaimed Mary as Queen, frustrating the Grey family's intention of proclaiming Jane in Aylesbury.

In nine days it was all over. The unfortunate Lady Jane Grey and her young husband were sent to the Tower and later executed. So the great Grey family, including the Lords of Wilton and Bletchley, had backed a loser, and Mary was crowned queen.

Before we take our final leave of Henry VIII and his tempestuous times, there is one other despatch to note – the despatch of the unfortunate last Abbot of Woburn, Robert Hobs. When Henry ordered the dissolution of Woburn Abbey, Abbot Hobs not unnaturally objected. But he also denied the King's supremacy in Church affairs. So he wasn't just despatched into the world to fend for himself – he was despatched at the end of a rope from the branches of an oak tree just outside the Abbey gates.

'Gunpowder, Treason and Plot'
From the Tudors on to the Stuarts, and to the first of their kings, James I. And that brings us to the Gunpowder Plot of November 5th 1605. The surface facts are soon told. Early in the morning of November 5th 1605 Guy Fawkes, a fanatical Catholic, was arrested in a cellar underneath the Houses of Parliament. With him were found thirty-six barrels of gunpowder, and the necessary fuses to explode them. The aim without doubt had been to blow up King James I, his wife, his heirs and his Parliament. At least some of the plotting to do this had been done at Gayhurst.

The impressive mansion at Gayhurst was new – its erection only began in 1597. The original 16th century Manor House had been given to Sir Francis Drake on his return from his voyage round the world. He later sold it to William Mulsoe who began

*Gayhurst Manor, where Guy Fawkes and Everard Digby planned the
Gunpowder Plot. It was given in 1581 to Sir Francis Drake after he had
sailed round the world, but he sold it a day later.*

to build the present house on the same site in 1597. Everard
Digby acquired the house by marriage. The Bucks. historian,
Lipscomb, says he had been educated by Catholic priests. The
house was certainly a safe haven for proscribed Catholics. It
had a secure secret hiding place for a Catholic priest, reached
through a cleverly designed swivelling floor leading to a
chamber below.

Everard Digby knew all about the plot to blow up
Parliament. At first he was reluctant to become involved,
especially because the plot was intended to destroy the king as
well as his Parliament. King James had, after all, knighted him.
But in the end he agreed. He entertained Guy Fawkes at
Gayhurst, and details of the plot were worked out. Sir Everard
Digby put up £1,500 to help pay for it. The plot failed. Sir
Everard Digby of Gayhurst along with others was arrested, and
on January 30th 1606 was hung drawn and quartered.

Civil War

A particular rite of passage happened in 1625 which was neither birth, marriage or death. It was the coronation of the first Stuart King, Charles I. A coronation is a very special event – a compound of national splendour, pageantry and solemnity. It is almost sacramental in the words and in the actions which accompany them. The coronation service has basically changed very little in nearly a thousand years. Three elements come together at a coronation – the people, the Church, and the monarch – each with their own part to play. The people acclaim, the Church blesses, and the monarch by oath undertakes to rule justly. So the new monarch is put in place, and all is well if all three elements are in harmony.

Before Charles was crowned in 1625 there had been twenty-four coronations in the nearly six hundred years going back to the time of William I. The reign of King John (1199–1216) had shown the strains that could result if King and people were at odds. The reign of Henry VIII had shown the strains that could result if King and Church were at odds. The reign of Charles I was to show the same strains if King and Parliament were at odds.

These strains were the more marked because Charles I believed firmly in the doctrine of the Divine Right of Kings. 'The King can do no wrong.' Within four years of his coronation he had quarrelled with Parliament over matters of finance, religion, and foreign policy. He dissolved Parliament in 1629 and for eleven years ruled his kingdom without it. But a threatened rebellion in Scotland, and his need for finance, forced Charles to recall Parliament. From then on the battle was joined between them, turning into outright civil war which lasted from 1642 to 1649.

Buckinghamshire was one of the first counties that joined in an association for mutual defence on the side of Parliament. The Buckinghamshire MP, John Hampden, became a national hero for opposing the Ship-money Tax. His regiment, the Greencoats, assembled at Aylesbury.

In all parts tenant farmers followed their landlords into either camp. No part of the kingdom escaped the effects of the seven years of civil war. Altogether there were twenty-two battles on English soil in which more than five thousand men were involved. Some one hundred thousand men were killed in the fighting. Astonishingly, that means that as a proportion of the total population, the one hundred thousand killed in the Civil War was probably a higher proportion than those who died in World War I. Though the great majority of the people was not caught up directly in the military campaigns, life was everywhere disrupted. Family was turned against family, and even members in the same family could find themselves on opposing sides.

The armies of both sides had perforce to live off the land, so the arrival of troops, whether Roundhead or Cavalier, threatened great loss, even ruin, to the populace on whom they descended. There are countless stories of wanton pillage and destruction perpetrated by both sides. One in seven of all the clergy in Buckinghamshire were ejected from their livings, among them the incumbents of Stony Stratford, Shenley, Moulsoe, Newton Longville, Great and Little Brickhill, Winslow and Beachampton. Some were ejected by Parliament because they were suspected of sympathy with Rome; others because they couldn't preach or neglected their parishes. Some were ejected by the Royalists because they wouldn't conform to strict Church of England rules.

Those seven years of civil war brought no really great battles to North Bucks. There was a fair-sized battle at Aylesbury and there were skirmishes at Fenny Stratford, Newport Pagnell and Olney. (Incidentally there was a young eighteen year old trooper in the Parliamentary Garrison at Newport Pagnell who was later to make a name for himself – he was John Bunyan.) There was lots of pillage and destruction in such places as Swanborne, Great Horwood and Buckingham for example.

In North Bucks. support for both sides was fairly evenly balanced. Aylesbury was firmly held by the Parliamentarians

Dinton Manor, home of a regicide.

who also held the strategic ridge of the Brickhills to deny the Royalists the way to London. There never was a Battle of Great Brickhill but it is interesting to speculate what might have happened if Prince Rupert and his cavalry had tried to dash up the Watling Street to the capital.

Perhaps the most moving individual episode of the civil war to impinge on our local history was the death at the Battle of Edgehill in 1642 of Sir Edmund Verney of Claydon. He was the Royal Standard bearer and lost his life in that battle. (See page 45.)

One hundred thousand deaths, and so much other suffering flowed from that rite of passage in 1625 when a king was crowned who believed so firmly that his coronation conferred on him Divine Right so that 'the King could do no wrong'. And it led him to execution on a cold January morning in Whitehall in January 1649.

That execution was carried out because twenty-six men signed the death warrant. Nine of them came from Bucks. One of them, Richard Deane of Princes Risborough, rose to high office under Cromwell. He was killed in a naval action off the North Foreland in 1653 and was buried with much honour in Henry VII's Chapel in Westminster Abbey.

In 1660 the monarchy was restored and Charles II ascended the throne of his late father. At once the hunt was on for the regicides, those twenty-six men who had signed the death warrant. Some had already died, others had fled the country. But nine were arrested, tried and executed. Simon Mayne of Dinton escaped execution but only because he died in the Tower in 1661. And Richard Deane, who had been buried with such honour in Westminster Abbey, suffered the indignity of having his remains disinterred and removed from the Abbey.

'The Sage of Hartwell'
So far we have seen how rites of passage – births, marriages and deaths, of our own national leaders have had their effects of local history. In 1789 there began that great upheaval across the Channel called the French Revolution. That too was to affect North Bucks.' history. In 1793 the French King, Louis XVI, and his wife, Marie Antionette, were executed. The Bourbon dynasty was abruptly terminated and the surviving members of the French Royal family went into exile. That exile took the future Louis XVIII first to Russia. But negotiations were started for him to find asylum in Britain. The Government offered him the use of Holyrood Palace in Edinburgh, but he wanted to be in London, or at least near the capital. A temporary home was provided for him at Stowe while somewhere more permanent could be found. That more permanent home was found – just outside Aylesbury at Hartwell House.

So the French court-in-exile came to North Bucks., and soon upwards of one hundred and fifty French people formed the court of the exiled Bourbon leader at Hartwell House. The future Louis XVIII was a quiet dignified figure who came to be dubbed 'The Sage of Hartwell'.

In due time, after the overthrow of Napoleon, Louis was able to return to France and the Bourbons resumed their rule. So came to an end the strange little chapter in North Bucks. history of the French enclave at Hartwell House.

But there was to be post-script, and again Stowe was involved. Louis Philippe, Duke of Orleans, who had been appointed King of France in 1830, was forced to abdicate. He went into exile, first in America, but later at Stowe where he lived for many years, and where he died.

But there is one final rite of passage of a quite different sort which has certainly had an enormous effect of local history. In fact it has completely transformed it. It was the passing of the Act of Parliament in 1965 which brought to birth the new city of Milton Keynes.

Chapter 5

THE HAND OF WAR

The year 1642 brought gloom to the whole nation, and personal tragedy to the Verney family at Claydon. In January, following the King's failure to arrest the five members in Parliament, King and Commons were on collision course, which could only lead to civil war. And in April Dame Margaret, wife to Sir Edmund Verney, died suddenly at Claydon.

Edmund Verney was appalled at the course the King was taking, yet so great was his loyalty to the throne that he stifled his fears. He was, after all, the King's right-hand man, the Royal Knight Marshall, and Standard Bearer to His Majesty. His Majesty, therefore, must be supported and obeyed. It is said that Sir Edmund quarreled with his own son over the King's action. His son seemed to accept that war was not only inevitable but also necessary. 'Without war there can be no justice and without justice I cannot face peace'. To this his troubled father could only reply: 'I understand what you say, but I have eaten the King's salt' . . . Sir Edmund's deep unhappiness increased still further when Dame Margaret, his wife, died in April. Her death shattered Sir Edmund, who never fully recovered from the blow. The nation's woes, and the loss of his wife combined to make that summer of 1642 a time of unrelieved depression for him.

The King was in the north with his followers. Refused admittance to Hull, he turned southwards again to Nottingham. There, on 22 August, he set up his Standard. Elsewhere Royalists and Parliamentarians tasted both success and failure. Dover and Portsmouth were lost to the King, but his nephew, the dashing Prince Rupert, routed the Roundheads at Powick Bridge near Worcester.

Verney Falls at Edgehill

By the last week of October the main Royalist Army was assembled on the high ground of Edgehill near Banbury – nearly four thousand mounted troops and over ten thousand foot soldiers, with the King in their midst. And at his side Sir Edmund Verney of Claydon, his Royal Standard Bearer. Ten miles away the Parliamentary Army was massed in strength at Kineton, under its Commander, the Earl of Essex. The two armies were numerically about equal. The Royalists had more horse, but the Parliamentary Army was superior in arms and equipment. The King's position on Edgehill was wellnigh impregnable – but was a defensive position what he needed? Immune from attack he might be, but strategically what he needed was the chance to sweep down from Edgehill to rout the enemy and then to make for London with all possible speed.

At 3pm on that fateful October day the battle was joined. The Royalist Cavalry charged under Prince Rupert. In the event, this was both glorious and foolish – glorious because the charge swept aside the Parliamentary lines, but foolish because, instead of wheeling to the left, where they could have had the Roundhead reserve and centre at their mercy, they continued their headlong charge straight ahead.

Meanwhile the King was left without his mounted guard, which had been given permission to charge at the head of Rupert's cavalry, So the King was undefended except for a small number of his personal footguard. Soon the infantry were locked in combat 'at push of pike'. The Royalist left wing wavered and the Roundheads pressed home their advantage. The King's Battle Standard was now the focus of the action. Sir Edmund Verney, firmly holding the Standard, was surrounded by a throng of his enemies. They offered him his life if he surrendered the Standard, but he answered above the roar of the battle: 'My life is my own, but the Standard is mine and my

Sovereign's, and I will not deliver it while I live.' To wrest the Standard from him they had to hack off the hand that held it. So the gloved right hand of the King's right-hand man was trampled underfoot, and so fell Sir Edmund Verney.

In the dusk of the October day the King himself was nearly captured, and was saved only by the timely arrival of some of Rupert's returning cavalry. Both sides were now exhausted, and when darkness fell the fighting ceased. At daybreak next morning the Royalists still held Edgehill Ridge. The enemy, despite the arrival of reinforcements, retired northwards, leaving the King undisputed master of the field of Edgehill.

Within the week the Royalists occupied Oxford and the King made that city his capital. The Roundheads established themselves at Aylesbury, and were thus in a position to deny the King a return to London.

Sir Edmund's body was not found after the Battle of Edgehill, but two different traditions afterwards emerged. The first tradition has it that a hand and arm of Sir Edmund were found among the slain on the battlefield and that these were later buried at Pendley in Hertfordshire. This was an estate which had formerly been in the possession of the Verney family. Certainly earlier Verneys had been buried there. But there are no records at Pendley to support the story; and Aldbury, the Parish which includes Pendley, is also silent on the subject.

The second tradition says that only Sir Edmund's hand – that which had held the Royal Standard – was found among the slain after the battle. The hand was identified by the ring on its little finger. The ring, still in the possession of the Verney family, is of fine gold. It carries a small oval crystal on which is painted a minute portrait of King Charles. The ring had been given to Sir Edmund by the King.

There is a third tradition too – a quaint one which says of Sir Edmund that 'he was neither born nor buried'. The reasoning behind this saying is, first, that he was 'never born' because his birth had been by Caesarian operation and that his mother had died in the process; and second, that since his body had never

46

Sir Edmund Verney's Monument at Claydon. Why did some say he was 'never born and never buried'?

been found after the battle, he had no known burial.

There is, then, no certain tomb for Sir Edmund. But there is a splendid memory. His loyalty and affection for his King cost him his life. And seven years later, on a cold January morning in 1649, that King would die too, executed in Whitehall.

Addison was right, then, when he wrote of Sir Edmund that he died *'greatly falling, with a falling State'*.

Claydon House today.
There have been Verneys in Buckinghamshire since the 13th century and at Claydon since the 15th century. The West Front, shown here, dates from the 18th century.
Sir Edmund Verney's monument is in the nearby Church.

Chapter 6

OF GRAVE CONCERN

'Our churchyards are one of our priceless and unique heritages. They contain a rich and relatively untapped source of vernacular art in which imaginative skill and craftsmanship in lettering, sculpture, and the use of local materials have combined to produce an almost infinite range of memorials, the like of which cannot be found in any other country. Generations of our ancestors are commemorated quietly, expansively, sadly, humorously, whimsically, eccentrically, and quite often anonymously.'

So says Geoffrey Knight in his little book 'Discovering Epitaphs'.

Throughout the Middle Ages only the wealthy had memorials. The poor were simply buried in the churchyard, one on top of another, over the centuries. An eight hundred year old churchyard, even assuming only six burials a year, could contain 4,800 bodies!

Custom, and a certain amount of ecclesiastical law control churchyards. Superstition has played its part too. For instance, the oldest graves are usually found to the south of the church, so as to avoid the shadow of the church falling on them. The Devil, ancient superstition reckoned, lurked among shadows and it was always supposed that he entered a churchyard from the north. So in many cases the north side wasn't used for burials if it could be avoided.

Headstones, traditionally, were placed at the head or western end of the grave. That way, it was thought, the eyes of the deceased could face the rising sun. Even in churchyards where this is not the case, all the headstones invariably face the same way.

An alternative to a headstone is a simple horizontal slab, called a ledger. The ledger was usually laid flat on the ground. But a refinement was to raise it up. Such raised slabs are called table or altar tombs.

It is what is inscribed on headstone or ledger that interests later generations. These inscriptions can be terse and factual, verbose and fulsome, solemn or humorous, sermonic and hortatory.

A good example of the hortatory is found in Wing Church:

> *'Honest old Thomas Cotes, that Sometimes was Porter at Ascott Hall, hath now, alas, left his Key, Lodge, Fyre, Friends and all to have a room in Heaven. This is that good man's grave.*
> > *Reader, prepare for thine*
> > *For none can tell*
> > *But that you two may meete tonight.*
> > *Farewell!'*

A good example of a sermonic memorial is to be found in Holy Trinity Church, Old Wolverton. The only snag is that it is all in Latin! However, here is a translation of what it says:

> *Sacred to the memory. Hard by lies Thomas Longueville of Wolverton, in the County of Bucks., Baronet, who after a second and happy marriage of a few months (with Catherine, second daughter and heiress of Thomas Peyton, of the County of Cambridge, Baronet) bowed to his fate on June 25th 1685, aged 54. Behold reader, no common ashes, sprung from an illustrious stock and ancient family, always in the king' service, ever faithful. There has died a good man, much to be desired as long as the following qualities are valued by mankind, viz sincere piety towards God, loyalty towards the needy, the strictest temperance and pleasing manners. By sudden*

death, God mercifully interrupted an excess of happiness lest his soul might decay and grow oblivious or unmindful of another heaven. There succeeded to the family title Edward (born of the former wife, Mary, daughter and co-heiress of William Fenwick of the County of Northumbria, Knight) the only son. Catherine, his very sad and dutiful wife, erected this monument to her dearly beloved husband.'

The habit in former centuries of recording memorial inscriptions in Latin is frustrating to most of us in these less classical times. The Latin memorial in St. Martin's Church, Fenny Stratford, commemorates Browne Willis, who built that church. It is believed to have been composed by Browne Willis himself. It is brief and convoluted, and even in English translation needs to be read carefully. In English translation it says:

*Here lies Browne Willis, Antiquarian,
to whose grandfather, Thomas Willis,
of everlasting memory, a leading physician
renowned throughout Europe
who died on St. Martin's Day AD 1675
this Chapel is a small memorial.
He expired on 3rd February AD 1760
in his 78th year.
O Christ, Saviour and Judge
be pitiful and merciful
to this man, greatest of sinners.'*

Humour on tombstones is usually frowned on by church authorities. For instance, when Robert Crews died in 1731 and was buried in Thame Church, his inscription ended with the words:
*'In the morning when sober
in the evening when mellow
you scarce ever met such
a jolly good fellow'.*

The Memorial to Browne Willis in Fenny Stratford Church takes a little sorting out!

The Bishop of Oxford, Samuel Wilberforce, irreverently known to some as 'Soapy Sam', ordered the words to be removed.

Yet in Dorchester Abbey this gem was allowed:

*'Here lies one who for medicine would not give
a little gold; and so his life he lost;
I fancy that he'd wish again to live
did he but know how much his funeral cost.'*

Quite often the trade or profession of the deceased is illustrated on his tombstone. Thus a gravestone at Hanslope commemorates Joseph Cox, who was a carpenter. On the stone are the arms of the Carpenters' Company, as well as the tools of his trade.

Not all burials were in the churchyard. It was customary for departed clergy to be interred inside the church, usually in the chancel. North Marston Church has a lovely example. The memorial stone, fixed to the north wall of the chancel, records the death of the Vicar, John Virgin, who died in 1694. In the bottom left-hand corner of the memorial is the carving of a hand, with a downward-pointing index finger. Round the pointing hand are inscribed, laconically, the words:

'He lise dust down thare'.

Ancient tombs of knights and lords are seen in many old churches. St. Mary's, Bletchley has a fine example. Where a recumbent Knight in armour lies on the top of his tomb, take a look at his legs. If they are crossed, you can know that he took

High on the outside wall of Chilton Church is the 13th century stone effigy of a Knight with crossed legs. He used to be inside till they altered the height of the nave roof in the 16th century.

53

part in one of the Crusades. If not, not.

Occasionally a tombstone tantalises by giving enough information to make one wonder, but not enough to satisfy one's curiosity. What do you suppose lies behind this couplet on a Luton headstone?

> *'Here lies the body of Thomas Procter*
> *who lived and died without a doctor.'*

And why does Richard Shrimpton's gravestone in High Wycombe Churchyard, dated 1727, carry the words:

> *'For being just unto a friend*
> *His enemies hastened his end'.*

Blessed John Schorne

Turning now from gravestone inscriptions to the actual persons buried beneath them, consider what happened to John Schorne, or rather, to his body. He was Vicar of North Marston from 1290 to 1314. When he died he was buried in North Marston

John Schorne's empty shrine in North Marston Church.

54

Church. Because of his enormous reputation for piety and good works, and for his renown in water-divining and healing the sick, and because it was said 'he conjured the Devil into a boot' – for all these reasons his grave in North Marston Church became a shrine. Soon hundred of pilgrims were making their way to the shrine of the blessed John Schorne. The North Marston shrine was said to be the third most popular in England, surpassed only by Walsingham and Canterbury.

Meanwhile the King was having thoughts about rebuilding St. George's Chapel in his Castle at Windsor. He summoned the

Pilgrims stayed here in North Marston until the Shrine was lost.

Bishop of Salisbury and told him to see to it.

The Bishop of Salisbury thought about it, and said to himself: 'What we need is a good set of bones!'. He meant that somehow he must attract pilgrims to Windsor in large numbers, and to do that he must have some saintly relics to cause them to come. The relics of John Schorne would do very nicely! Permission to remove John Schorne's remains was sought from the Pope, who consented. So the Shrine of John Schorne at North Marston was moved to Windsor and the lucrative pilgrim traffic followed it. St. George's Chapel at Windsor was completed to everyone's satisfaction, except possibly to the villagers of North Marston!

*But this pub still 'honours'
John Schorne's memory.*

Far back in history, before ever there were any churches or churchyards, there were burying places called barrows. The Dictionary defines a barrow as 'a heap of earth placed over one or more prehistoric tombs, often surrounded by ditches'.

There are two such barrows at Thornborough near Buckingham. They are grass-covered mounds very much higher than the surrounding land. In 1840 the Duke of Buckingham caused them to be investigated. The result was the discovery of the greatest set of Romano-British remains that had ever been discovered up to that time. The artefacts uncovered are now in the Archaeological Museum in Cambridge. There were discovered also traces of cremation burials, and evidence that on that spot in about 256 AD there had been a pre-christian temple. So the Thornborough barrows are in a sense churchyards of a sort too.

The Battle at Holman's Bridge

Move on several centuries, from 256 AD to 1818. In that year the bones of 247 people were found in pits four or five feet deep outside Aylesbury at a place called Holman's Bridge. A monument was erected on that spot to commemorate them. They were the men who had been killed in the Battle of Aylesbury in 1642 in the Civil War.

Belatedly but reverently the remains were disinterred and reburied in Hardwick Churchyard. It was Lord Nugent who arranged for this to be done. On a marble slab this inscription was engraved:

'Within are deposited the bones of two hundred and forty seven persons which were discovered AD 1818 buried in a field adjoining Holman's Bridge. From the history and appearance of the place where they were found, they are concluded to be the remains of those officers and men who perished in an engagement fought AD 1642 between the troops of Charles the First, under the command of Prince Rupert, and the garrison who held Aylesbury for the Parliament. Enemies, from their attachment to opposite leaders and to opposite standards in the sanguinary conflicts of that civil war, they were, together victims of its fury, united in one common slaughter. They were buried in one common grave close to the spot where they had lately stood in arms against each other. May the memory of the brave be respected, and may our country never again be called to take part in contests such as these which this tablet records'. And so say all of us! So today the remains of Cavaliers and Roundheads are united in Hardwick Churchyard. The enemies found common ground at last.

A year after the Battle of Aylesbury there was a lesser battle – little more than a skirmish, in 1643. It took place on and around Olney Bridge. The numbers of those killed is not known. But some of them, Cavaliers and Roundheads, lie buried together in the fields of Emberton.

On 20th November 1830 William Ovitts of Winslow died at the age of eighty-seven. He was buried on the south side of the tower of Winslow Parish Church. As a young man he had enlisted in Elliot's Regiment of Light Dragoons, a regiment that had been raised in 1758. It served on the continent in The Seven

Years War (1756–1763) and took part in the Battle of Freyburgh.

In the course of that battle the Hereditary Prince of Brunswick was captured by two French Dragoons and a Foot Soldier. Young Ovitts witnessed the incident and galloped after them. He killed all three Frenchmen and was severely wounded himself. But he rescued the Prince and brought him safely back. The grateful Prince rewarded his gallantry with a Purse of one hundred guineas. Ovitt's officers recommended his promotion but he refused, thinking his education standards were insufficient. The Duke of Buckingham, hearing of his courage, made him an allowance of one shilling a day for the rest of his life. So by the time he went to his grave in 1830, the Winslow hero had enjoyed his unusual pension for well over sixty years.

In the north aisle of Newport Pagnell Parish Church in 1619 the body of a man was dug up. The hollow parts of his bones were found to be full of lead. The whole interior of the cranium – the part of the skull that encloses the brain – was entirely filled with lead, which was taken to Cambridge and deposited in the Library of St. John's College.

And another grave at Newport Pagnell Parish Church has interesting and unexpected links with a grave in faraway Virginia, USA. Both are graves of members of the well-known Newport Pagnell Waller family.

John Waller died in Newport Pagnell in 1723. In his will, dated 1715, he had stipulated that when he died he was to be buried *'in that vault or monument which I caused to be built on the south side of the church at Newport Pagnell, which remains for a burying place for myself and those of my family of Wallers for ever'*.

But there had been another member of that family who was not destined to be buried in Newport Pagnell. His name was also John Waller and he had emigrated to Virginia, where he prospered. He made a fortune with his cotton fields, employed many slaves, and built himself a fine house and estate called 'Enfield'. There he died and was buried. He figures in Alex Haley's remarkable book, 'Roots', as the following passage testifies:

'. . . Colonel built dat Enfield, but he buried right here'
And walking outside the cook showed him the grave and
its lettered tombstone. She read the long since memorised
inscription: 'Sacred to the memory of Colonel John
Waller, Gentleman, third son of John Waller and Mary
Key who settled in Virginia in 1635, from Newport
Pagnell, Bucks.'

At first sight Granborough Churchyard in the Vale of Aylesbury has a gravestone more sensational than any that have figured in this chapter. The stone is over the grave of a lady who died in 1723. Its inscription informs the world that she died at the age of 232! However, she earns no place in any record book. The stonemason made a 'typing' error you might say. The lady died aged 23.

This gravestone in Granborough Churchyard says the lady died aged 232.
Just a stonemason's slip! She was 23.

59

How Many Died that Day?

In Holy Trinity Church at Drayton Parslow near Bletchley there is a memorial brass whose wording suggests at least a double tragedy and possibly even a multiple disaster. The brass is dated 1535 and is a memorial to Benet Blacknolle, his wife Agnes, and their fourteen children (three boys and eleven girls). The inscription reads:

> *'Of your charitie pray for the soules of*
> *Benet Blacknolle and Agnes his wife*
> *who died the XXX day of September*
> *MDXXXV. With the children's*
> *soules J'u have mercy. Amen.'*

It seems clear from this that Benet and Agnes Blacknolle died together – a double tragedy. But some have wondered whether perhaps the children also perished on that September day in 1535. It is just possible to reach that conclusion from the wording of the inscription. After four and a half centuries we can never know.

Memorial in Bierton Church, 1626 'He had by her nine sons and four daughters'. But the six in cots died in infancy.

Chapter 7

THE DRAGON OF WHADDON

That's what J G Jenkins called his biography of Browne Willis. The dragon in question was a remarkable man with a name to conjure with in Bucks., but further afield too. He claimed descent from a good solid yeoman family who in the time of Elizabeth I lived at Church Harborough in Oxfordshire. It was a family of sturdy loyalty to both Church and Throne. Browne Willis's great-grandfather lost his life in 1643 fighting for the Royalist cause at the siege of Oxford. And his grandfather became a figure of national importance and laid the foundations of the family fortune. He was Thomas Willis, a famous physician of Charles II's time who became Professor of Natural Philosophy at the Restoration. He is regarded as the founder of neurological science, and a pioneer in the study and treatment of diabetes. He lived in London in St. Martin's Lane and worshipped daily in St. Martin's Church before going out to visit his patients. If he ever had occasion to treat a patient on a Sunday he always gave the fees to charity. He died on St. Martin's Day, 1675. The young Browne Willis greatly revered his grandfather, though he never actually knew him. Browne Willis was born in 1682, seven years after the death of the great physician in 1675.

By an odd coincidence Browne Willis's father, another Thomas Willis, also died on St. Martin's Day, in 1699, at the early age of forty-one. All these appearances of St. Martin's Day in the lives of his nearest relatives were not lost on the dragon, as we shall see.

Browne Willis had his early education at Beachampton

This 18th century sketch of Browne Willis hangs in the Ringing Chamber of St. Martin's Church, Fenny Stratford.

School, from which he went on to Westminster School. He went up to the University of Oxford in 1700, staying there for four years but without taking a degree. As a young man he stayed as a guest and pupil in the Rectory of the village of Milton Keynes. The Rector, Dr Wotten, was a keen antiquarian and it was from him that the young Browne Willis acquired his interest in all things antiquarian, an interest which became an obsession for the rest of his life.

In 1674 the second Duke of Buckingham, to clear some of his debts, sold the Manor of Fenny Stratford to Thomas Willis, the neurologist. And in 1698 the second Thomas Willis, the dragon's father, also bought the Manor of Whaddon from the Duke. So it came about that when his father died in 1699, young Browne Willis, still a minor, inherited the three Manors of Bletchley, Fenny Stratford and Whaddon.

In 1707 Browne Willis married Catherine Elliott, who was herself a descendant of Walter Giffard, who had held those same Manors back in the 11th century. Catherine brought with her into her marriage with Browne Willis a fortune of £8,000. Ironically, the dragon was to waste £5,000 of this in a misguided effort to rebuild the Manor House at Whaddon, an architectural disaster which the next owner had to pull down.

The 13th Burgess

In 1705, two years before marrying Catherine, Browne Willis went into politics. He stood for election as MP for Buckingham. In those days election was not by universal suffrage but by an electoral college of Burgesses. In Buckingham there were thirteen such Burgesses. When election day came only twelve of them were present, and these voted six for Browne Willis and six for his opponent. Where was the thirteenth Burgess? The answer was that he was in prison for debt. So they hastily went to the Debtor's Prison, brought him out and asked him to cast his vote. He did so – for Browne Willis. Then they popped him back into prison again. So the dragon became MP for Buckingham and served as such for three years until 1708. There is no record that he ever spoke in the House.

When he was elected MP Browne Willis bought a bolt of blue cloth from which he had a greatcoat made. In itself that would not be worth recording, except that Browne Willis wore that greatcoat for the next fifty-five years, until he died in fact. It was patched and repatched countless times and he wore a great leather belt over it. He wore the same old boots for more than forty years too, and his wig, more brown that white, was equally disreputable. No wonder William Cole, the diarist Rector of Bletchley, described him as 'looking more like a mumping beggar than a gentleman'. Mind you, Cole himself sometimes dressed a little oddly too. Sir John Cullum wrote: 'The only time I had the pleasure of seeing him (Cole) he had as many envelopes as an onion. It was a very warm autumnal day when he came in a coach and four to dine. As soon as he was unpacked he threw off a rug surtout and entered the parlour invested with a waistcoat, coat, greatcoat, Master of Arts gown, and Hussar cloak, the inferior parts defended with boots, stockings and galoches'.

Antiquary, historian, author, squire, church patron and church builder, member of Parliament – the Dragon of Whaddon was all these. His published works number more than a dozen and include surveys of virtually all the Cathedrals of England and Wales. He made a notable collection of coins and tradesmen's tokens and presented the whole lot to Oxford University. The University, which he had left in 1704 without taking a degree, honoured him with an MA by Diploma in 1720, and in 1749 conferred on him the degree of DCL.

In the field of church building and restoration Browne Willis was a notable benefactor. He repaired Bletchley Church in 1704, gave it new bells in 1712, repaired Buckingham Church tower in 1752, and restored Bow Brickhill Church in 1756.

But above all he built St. Martin's Church, Fenny Stratford, between 1724 and 1730. Here he was able to express in bricks and mortar his devotion both to St. Martin and to his grandfather who had died on St. Martin's Day. And there, in 1760, he was buried.

Browne Willis was an eccentric who at all times cut a quaint figure. He could be quarrelsome too and was often fierce in controversy. On occasions he could be bigotted also. A good example of this is the action he took when someone had the temerity to open a non-conformist chapel in Fenny Stratford. Browne Willis promptly bought it, pulled it down, and used the materials from it to build stables at Whaddon Hall. Here is how he described his actions and the reasons for them in 1725:

> 'Dissenters from the C of E, taking advantage of these our unhappy circumstances, combined together, and a few years ago erected in our town a Meeting House or Conventicle to promote schism and separation from the true religion by Law established. But as this proved very disagreeable and unacceptable to us, so means were at length found to purchase, buy off, and pull down the said building thus by them erected, and security given under our hand & seals "not to dispose of for the future any of

our messuages, cottages, lands, tenements or hereditaments, or any part of them, nor any Barns, Outhouses or buildings whatsoever, to any person or persons whomsoever, for the erecting, building, raising or making any Meeting House or in any sort permit or suffer such Meeting House or Conventicle to be built, made, had, or used in or upon any of our premises".'

Clearly, then the dragon wanted no nonconformist church or chapel in Fenny Stratford. But what he did want above all was to give Fenny its own Parish Church. He himself later described the building and dedication of St. Martin's as his 'chiefest and most real worldly comfort and happiness'.

But how was it that Fenny didn't already have a parish church of its own? The answer is that it had always been part of the parish of St. Mary's, Bletchley. But Fenny had once possessed a place of worship, though it was not a parish church. It stood on that very site where Browne Willis would one day build St. Martin's Church. It was a Chantry Chapel, and by all accounts it had been a fairly substantial building, comprising a tower with bells, a nave and a chancel, and a churchyard. That Chantry Chapel, dedicated to St. Margaret and St. Catherine, was built as early as the 15th century. The earliest reference to it is that it was listed in 1460 as the VENY STRATFORD CAPELLA.

In 1494 a group of men applied for permission to establish a Chantry Guild which would use the Chapel of St. Margaret and St. Catherine for its worship. Such Guilds or Fraternities were often set up. They were religious foundations but were not monasteries. Those who joined them were not bound by monastic vows, but were individuals, both men and women, who chose to live under religious rules. The Guild founded in Fenny in 1494 required its members to pray regularly for the good estate of the king, and for the souls of Rogers and John Hobbes, the Founders. The guild was also responsible for providing two priests, 'to minister sacraments, there being 220 communicants in the said hamlet'.

Chantry House, behind The Bull in Fenny. Here lived the members of the Guild of St. Margaret and St. Catherine until the dissolution in 1547.

Members of the Guild lived in community on a site behind the Bull Inn on the Watling Street. Some of their timbered buildings survive and have now been restored as part of an office complex, appropriately called Chantry House.

The Guild lasted fifty-three years and the names of the nine priests who served Fenny during that time are on record. But then came the Reformation, and in 1547 Chantries and Chantry Guilds were everywhere abolished. For a short while the last two priests, Walter Wood and William Prestwick, were allowed to continue to minister in Fenny. But in 1553 the Chapel was sold to three London land speculators. It was pulled down and the materials carried off for use elsewhere.

So then Fenny Stratford, which had never had a parish church of its own, now didn't even have its Chantry Chapel. And that state of affairs continued for the next one hundred and seventy years until Browne Willis came along and changed it.

He began by buying the site of the old Chantry Chapel and then set to work to raise the money to build the new church. He already knew what its dedication would be – St. Martin's, of course, in memory of his revered grandfather.

At last there came the great day when the Bishop of Lincoln came to dedicate the new church. It was May 27th, 1730. What Browne Willis built, and what the Bishop of Lincoln dedicated that day is now just the north aisle of today's church. Nevertheless, no less than ninety clergy attended the Bishop's Visitation on the following morning, and in the afternoon an astonishing one thousand candidates were confirmed by the Bishop, coming from all the surrounding deaneries.

How should one sum up the extraordinary Browne Willis, the Dragon of Whaddon? He was certainly eccentric, often quarrelsome, fierce in controversy, and frequently bigoted. His own family felt that he spent far too much on his church benefactions, to the detriment of the family itself. But he was above all a great churchman, both a high Tory and a high Anglican, loyal to both Church and State. Let the last word on the dragon come from the priest who attended him on his death bed in 1760. That priest wrote:

'He was strictly religious without any mixture of superstition and enthusiasm. He was a constant frequenter of the Church and never absented himself from the Holy Communion. In the time of his health he called his family to prayers every evening. He had many valuable and good friends whose kindness to him he always acknowledged. And though perhaps he might have disputes with a few, the reason which it would be disagreeable to enter into, yet it is with satisfaction that I can affirm that he was perfectly reconciled with everyone'.

Chapter 8

BRIDGES . . . and TROUBLED WATERS

Milton Keynes has a prodigious number of bridges, and is adding to their number. They are all shapes and sizes, serving a variety of purposes. There are bridges over rivers and canals; bridges over roads and railways; railway bridges over roads and canals; and bridges carrying water over water.

Canal mania from 1793 to 1805 gave North Bucks. a great number of bridges. The length of the Grand Union Canal between Fenny Stratford and Stony Stratford is thirteen miles, and it has the same number of bridges. Some of them are the picturesque hump-back type – interesting as survivors, but hazardous for traffic of a kind of undreamt of when they were erected.

Aqueducts are also bridges. The best-known aqueduct in North Bucks. is The Iron Trunk. It carries the Grand Union Canal across the valley of the River Ouse at Old Wolverton. It was the work of William Jessup. His first attempt was built of stone and collapsed in 1808. His second attempt, The Iron Trunk, was and is a spectacular success, still safely carrying canal traffic across the valley nearly two hundred years later.

A tiny, almost unknown aqueduct at Water Eaton carries the same canal over the small Cottenham Stream which is a tributary of the Ouzel on its way in turn to become a tributary of the Ouse.

And history was made in July 1991 when a new £4 million aqueduct was opened in the heart of Milton Keynes. It is 120 metres long and carries the Canal over the Grafton Street dual-carriageway. So the two hundred year old canal now has a

The Iron Trunk has safely carried the Grand Union Canal over the valley for nearly 200 years. But the first version collapsed in 1808.

new aqueduct – the first to be built for half a century. Running alongside it is not only a towpath, but also yet another length of Milton Keynes' celebrated Redway system for pedestrians and cyclists.

Just as the canal-building boom caused a spate of bridge building, so too did the coming of the railways. The resultant bridges and viaducts are not the loveliest things to look at. One of them, carrying the railway from Bletchley to Oxford, dominates part of Bletchley, almost cutting it in half. That line carries only freight now, but a campaign is in progress to re-open it to passenger traffic.

What Jessup was to canal building, Robert Stephenson was to railway construction. His special claim to fame as a railway engineer was his designing and construction of 'skew' bridges. There are two notable examples in Milton Keynes. Though neither please the eye of the ordinary beholder, both excite engineers and railway buffs. One of them carries the line over the old Stony Stratford/Newport Pagnell turnpike road (the 'Old Road' in Wolverton).

The other great 'skew' bridge is Denbigh Bridge, carrying the railway line over the busy A5, the Watling Street, in Bletchley. It was here that Bletchley's first railway station was sited in 1838. In fact, for some months that year the line from Euston terminated here. Passengers had then to take the stage-coach on to Rugby where they could resume their rail journey to Birmingham. That 'hiccup' was cured when the tunnel at Kilsby was completed, enabling the railway to run right through from London to the Midlands. But for nearly a year Denbigh assumed an importance it would soon lose. Contemporary accounts make it clear that it was a shambles. There was a pub there called Denbigh Hall which had a bonanza when the railway came. But there was little else by way of amenities to cater for the travelling public. Huts and shanties sprang up all around, and for a while all was chaos.

In architectural terms a 'skew arch' is an arch whose line is not at right angles to its abuttments. It was the genius of Robert Stephenson to achieve this with his railway bridges. He first made a wooden model of each skew bridge, and when the real thing was put in hand, all went into place faultlessly.

Undoubtedly the most important road bridge in Milton Keynes was that over the River Ouse at Stony Stratford. The trouble was – who should maintain it? The Parishes and local Turnpike Trusts could disclaim responsibility for it. It took an Act of Parliament in 1801 to try to sort out the problem. But the Act was very unpopular and met sustained resistance. Not until 1833 was a solution found. The proposal then was that the Trustees under the 1801 Act should be relieved of responsiblity for the bridge, in return for a payment by them of £900. The Government would then rebuild the bridge and maintain it thereafter. A second Act was passed to this effect in 1834, and construction of the new bridge began at once. It was completed by July 1835. But local wrath was still occasioned by the system of Tolls which the Government introduced. It took another twenty years for the Toll gates and Toll houses to be removed.

Stony Stratford Bridge over the Ouse, built in 1835. Its predecessors saw many notable floods.

Pride of Newport Pagnell

Telford has its Iron Bridge – *the* Iron Bridge – the first anywhere in the world. But vehicles can no longer cross it, only pedestrians. On the other hand, Newport Pagnell also has an Iron Bridge, Tickford Bridge, named after Tickford Priory. Whereas Telford's Iron Bridge is deservedly a jewell in the complex of industrial museums at Telford, Newport Pagnell's cast-iron bridge is a good, honest, everyday working bridge. It is the oldest working cast-iron bridge in the country – possibly the oldest in the world. Ever since 1810 it has spanned the River Lovatt, carrying traffic which has 'progressed' from horsedrawn to horseless. Only one other bridge like Tickford Bridge exists – and that is in Spanish Town, Jamaica.

71

Tickford Bridge, the pride of Newport Pagnell, built in 1810 – the oldest working cast-iron bridge in Britain.

No catalogue of North Bucks. bridges would be complete without mentioning the loveliest of all. It is not only the loveliest but also the last surviving medieval bridge in the whole of Buckinghamshire. It spans Claydon Brook, a tributary of the Ouse, where the busy A421 road from Bletchley approaches Buckingham.

It was built near Thornborough in the 14th century of lovely honey-coloured stone. Until just a few years ago it continued to carry busy 20th century traffic over its six arches. Then the A421 was realigned so as to pass within a few yards of the grand old bridge, rewarding the passing motorist with a sight of it as he goes on his way. It has stood for nearly five hundred years already. Now that only pedestrians can cross it, there seems no reason why it should not last another five hundred years.

'Like a bridge over troubled waters . . .'

so went a popular song a generation or so ago. Local history provides plenty of stories of troubled waters.

Thornborough Bridge over Claydon Brook – the oldest medieval bridge in Bucks. Good for another 500 years.

The Ouse and its tributaries – Cottenham, Lovatt, Loughton and Ouzel – occupy a fairly modest position in the league table of English river systems. All the same, their waters have caused trouble enough in past centuries. Markham wrote of them as looking occasionally like a raging sea. He cites one flood in particular when on 8th November 1823, the waters came over both causeway and bridge at Stony Stratford; coaches were overturned and horses drowned.

Many a time in past centuries Fenny Stratford would be cut off from Water Eaton by floods. One flood was so bad that it earned an entry in Bletchley Parish Register:

'June 6th Day. There was a Great Flood at Water Eaton that was so Big that the Like hath not bin seen by all Mens knolidge this fore Hundren year be fore. It was in 1725.'

A similar flood in 1693 cost the life of the Rector of Milton Keynes. The Reverend Lewis Atterbury was swept away and drowned as he attempted to cross the bridge at Newport Pagnell.

Even when the floods were not extensive, the mud could be a great hazard, and trying to cross a bog could make a nightmare of a journey. In an 1810 publication (A General View of Agriculture in Buckinghamshire) the author wrote:

> 'The bye roads of Bucks. are extremely bad . . . they have ruts so deep that when the wheels of the chaise fall into them . . . the horse and chaise must inevitably fall into bogs. Finding the way from Fenny Stratford to Whaddon (through Water Eaton) was such that without a guide I could not have surmounted it. From Winslow to Wing there was no less danger, and had it not been for a colony of gypsies I might have been obliged to have taken refuge in a milking-house for a night's lodging.'

No more graphic account of the perils of floods could better that recorded in 1823 in his Parish Register by the Reverend Henry Gauntlett, Vicar of Olney:

> 'Account of the rapid rise of the Ouse on Thursday and Friday, October the thirtieth and thirty-first, 1823, with the providential escape of two young men who were exposed to its peril.
>
> On Thursday October the thirtieth, after some moderate showers in the morning, it began to rain about noon with considerable violence, and continued through the whole of that day and night, and the greater part of the next day. The flood began to rise on Thursday night, and continued rapidly to increase till about one o'clock am on Saturday morning when it had risen to a height never before remembered or recorded. At this time it covered the bridge from one end to the other with the exception of the high arches over the mill-stream. From

that period it began gradually to subside and in the course of two or three days entirely disappeared.

On Friday evening the road between Olney and Emberton became impassable. About 8 o'clock two young men, Isaac Young, an apprentice to Mrs Smith, Grocer of Olney, in the twenty-first year of his age, and William Smith, son of the same, in his nineteenth year, attempted to pass from Emberton to Olney in a covered cart. Near the Emberton Bridge they were borne away by the current and drifted in the cart to a hedge by the roadside. There the water was exceedingly deep and the horse was soon drowned, being confined by the cart and the hedge in which he was entangled. One of the young men with great difficulty got into the top of a willow tree in the midst of the hedge; and the other, William Smith, with scarcely less difficulty gained the tilt of the cart.

Their alarming situation was discovered by the inhabitants of Emberton through the information of two persons who in another cart returned to that place having made a fruitless and dangerous attempt to pass to Olney. The night was quite dark and the wind very high, yet two persons of Emberton with a noble boldness endeavoured to wade to the young men; but having nearly lost their own lives, they were obliged to return, leaving as it was feared the poor sufferers to a watery grave.

No boat could be obtained, nor any means devised to meet the case. The youths however continued in their situation, occasionally expecting that the waves would wash away the cart, and tear up the willow tree by its roots. They were cheered every hour by the appearance of lights carried towards them by the inhabitants of Emberton, who endeavoured by this means and by their voices to keep up their spirits. Owing however to the howling of the wind the latter means of encouragement was of no avail, as their voices were not heard by the sufferers. One of the young men was very pious and by

*midnight, amidst the winds and the dashing of the
waters, he sang with his companion Cowper's beautiful
hymn:*

*"God moves in a mysterious way
His wonders to perform,
He plants His footsteps in the sea
And rides upon the storm"*

*The next morning another attempt at deliverance was
made which succeeded. The young men were rescued and
led out of danger, and being put into comfortable beds at
Emberton, they were soon refreshed by a sweet sleep and
in a short time recovered their strength.*

*By the rapid rise of this flood some lives were lost in
various places, and many were in jeopardy. A
considerable number of cattle also perished.'*

The records show that in that same flooding following the
severe storm of 1823, more than five hundred sheep were
drowned between Winslow and Buckingham.

Floods can be terrifying and ruinous. But, as Noah found
quite a long time ago, they do not last for ever. As Wordsworth
wrote back in 1807:

*'There was a roaring in the wind all night;
The rain came heavily and fell in floods;
But now the sun is rising, calm and bright'.*

Chapter 9

SAINTS PRESERVE US !

Some of the churches in our area date back to the 11th century or even before. Perhaps pride of place should be given to All Saints Church in Brixworth in Northamptonshire. It has been described as 'the finest 7th century church north of the Alps'.

For nine hundred years many of our churches have been built, enlarged, altered and restored. Some have been pulled down altogether and replaced on the same site. And some, surprisingly few, have been declared redundant.

All of them have names. The idea of attaching names, usually of saints, to places of worship seems to have started in Rome perhaps as early as the 4th century. From then on, wherever the church spread, that custom accompanied it.

We commonly say that a church is 'dedicated' to St. Someone-or-other. Technically that is wrong. The church is dedicated to God, and in honour of St. Someone-or-other. But let's not be pedantic. We know what we mean when we say the church is dedicated to this or that saint.

Firmin

But what we don't always know is who the saint was. There's no problem with St. John's, St. Peter's, St. James and so on. And even less problem with churches called Christ Church, Holy Trinity, All Saints and the like. But how about *St. Firmin's*? You don't know who St. Firmin was? Don't feel guilty. Even in North Crawley they are not too sure, and their church is St. Firmin's. (There is only one other St. Firmin's in England and that is at Thurlby up in Lincolnshire.)

St. Firmin's Church, North Crawley is actually named in the Domesday Book of 1086. Now there was a very early French Bishop called Firmin. He was martyred in about 209 AD and buried at Amiens. Was the church in North Crawley named in his honour? One might suppose so, except for one thing. The 12th century Peterborough Chronicle mentions the relics of a St. Firmin being moved from a monastery at North Crawley to Thorney. So it is possible that the founder of the small North Crawley Saxon monastery was a Firmin. In other words, the church there is dedicated to a local saint of that name, rather than to the other Firmin back in France in the 3rd century.

Nothing at all remains of the first North Crawley Saxon church. It was replaced by a small Norman church, which in turn was enlarged over the succeeding centuries. One such enlargement at the end of the 13th century involved the rebuilding of the chancel. This was the work of Peter of Guildford who became Rector in 1294. He marked the alteration in touching fashion with a memorial stone on which are inscribed (in Latin) the words:

'Peter gives to thee, O Firmin, a new little
Chancel, in order that when you praise God
you may remember Peter'.

Guthlac
If you were bemused by St. Firmin, how do you feel about *St. Guthlac*? Who was he? And why is the church in Passenham named in his honour?

The answer to the first question is that Guthlac was a younger member of the Royal House of the Saxon Kingdom of Mercia in the early 8th century. But he forsook the life at court and went off to live as a hermit. Later his piety was recognised and he was canonised.

Passenham, Deanshanger and Puxley are all Saxon place names, and it is very likely that there was a small wooden Saxon church at Passenham at the beginning of the 10th century. So it is not strange that it was named in honour of a

St. Helen, nother of the first Christian Emperor, Constantine, in Broughton Church's fine medieval murals. She is reputed to have found the remnants of the true Cross.

local saint with royal connections.

Passenham was (and still is) a very small place. But it was mentioned by name in the Saxon Chronicle as early as 921 AD, when the Saxon King Edward the Elder camped there with his army.

By the time of Henry I (1100–1135) there had already been a church at Passenham dedicated to St. Guthlac for a long time. From the 12th to the 16th century it came under the Abbey at Cirencester.

Next door to the church stands Passenham Manor. Lord of the Manor in the 17th century was the redoubtable Robert Banastre, a man of very mixed reputation. He is buried in the chancel of the church, and his monument, affixed to the wall above his tomb, tells how he 'built and beautified this Faire Chauncell'.

He paid for extensive murals of prophets and evangelists to be painted, and he commissioned elaborately carved and decorated stalls, and a magnificent Jacobean pulpit.

The murals were 'lost' under whitewash for almost two centuries, but were rediscovered in the nineteen-fifties when restoration work was being done on the Jacobean carved stalls. So the murals were restored and the work was completed by 1966.

Rumbold

The old parish church of Buckingham was built in the 13th century, with a fine spire rising 163 feet. The church was dedicated in honour of St. Peter and St. Paul. In 1698 the spire fell, damaging the tower. It was repaired, but in 1776 it fell again. So the whole building was demolished and replaced by a new parish church on a better site. A feature of the old church was a south transept called 'St. Rumbold's Aisle', containing the chapel and shrine of the legendary saint of Buckingham. So who was St. Rumbold? There is much that's odd about him. In the first place the spelling of his name varies from Rumbold to Rumwold. It is generally agreed that he was born in 626 AD. His father was King of Northumberland and his mother was a daughter of Penda, the pagan King of Mercia.

Rumbold (Rumwold) was baptised as an infant and died shortly afterwards. That wouldn't have made him unique, but legend says that at his own infant baptism he clearly and loudly professed his faith. It is said, too, that when he was only three days old he preached a splendid sermon to his parents!

If Rumbold (Rumwold) had been baptised as an adult, all this would be both credible and creditable – a new Christian standing up for his faith in a largely pagan world. But no – legend said firmly that he was born, baptised, and died, all in the same year, 626 AD.

The same legend related that he left clear instructions about his own burial. He was to be buried for a year at King's Sutton; then interred for three years at Brackley; and finally buried for ever in Buckingham.

After his death he was canonised as a Saint. There is a mention of him at least once, in a Church Calendar dated 1000 AD. Elsewhere in England at least two churches were built and dedicated in his honour. But not at Buckingham.

The reputation of St. Rumbold (Rumwold) was such that many pilgrims flocked to visit his shrine in Buckingham, and several wells named after him were said to have water that gave relief to the lame and blind. To accommodate the pilgrims a large inn or hotel was built at the west end of the church and was known as The Pilgrim's Inn. Today St. Rumbold's Street and Well Street in Buckingham near the old churchyard serve as a kind of memorial to the legendary and saintly baby.

Frideswide

If St. Guthlac and St. Rumbold are examples of saint-making dating from long before the Conquest, we should notice a third example too. The church at Plough Corner, Water Eaton, is dedicated to *St. Frideswide.*

St. Frideswide was the daughter of an 8th century Mercian prince who lived at Oxford. At an early age she became a nun and founded a convent, which in later years was given to Augustinian canons. The convent was later acquired by Wolsey who applied its proceeds to his Cardinal College in Oxford. That College later became part of Christ Church. Its 12th century chapel is the present Oxford Cathedral. How amazed Frideswide would have been at what happened to her little nunnery.

It is said that Algar, a neighbouring prince, had wanted to marry Frideswide, being much impressed by her beauty. When she refused him and said that she was going to become a nun, he invaded Oxford with an army. Frideswide escaped down the river in a boat and hid in the woods near Abingdon. Algar later went blind, and legend has it that his sight was restored through the prayers of Frideswide. Another legend about St. Frideswide tells how by her prayer a fountain sprang up at Binsey in Oxford. St. Frideswide's Well is still to be seen there today. Lewes Carrol told Alice it was a Treacle Mine (anticipating Ken Dodd's delightful fantasy about Jam Butty mines by more than a century). St. Frideswide's tomb became a very popular place of pilgrimage. Her feast day is kept on October 19th.

Faith

How about *St. Faith*? There are about twenty-six churches in England bearing this dedication, and one of them is at Newton Longville near Bletchley. St. Faith was a child martyr, burned to death in the persecution under Diocletian in about 304 AD. When accused of being a christian she was told she could save her life if she recanted. She refused and was burnt to death on a brazen grate. She is generally represented in art with a palm branch and a grate.

At the Conquest, as William extended his hold over the whole country, he rewarded his followers and supporters with Manors. To Walter Giffard were given Manors in North Bucks. Like many other Lords of the Manor, Walter Giffard built churches. But at Newton Longville he did more – he founded a Priory, and linked it with a Mother House in France. That Mother House was the Cluniac Priory of St. Faith at Longueville in Normandy. The Priory at Newton was always a small house. During the One Hundred Years War all such 'alien' priories were closed down. However, the residents of Newton Longville still worship in St. Faith's Church, and in recent years have cultivated fraternal links with the Church and Priories in Normandy.

Giles

Up and down England there are well over one hundred and fifty churches dedicated to *St. Giles*. One of them is in Stony Stratford. Giles was an Abbot in Provence who died in about 720 AD. They have his relics in Toulouse. He is said to be Patron Saint of cripples and beggars. In the Middle Ages he was an immensely popular saint, which is why so many churches bear his name.

The popular story about him relates how he withdrew from society to live as a hermit in a cave on the banks of the Rhone. For sustenance he relied on the herbs of the field and the milk of a tame hind. One day the king passed by on a hunting expedition. His huntsmen and hounds pursued the tame hind right up to the cave where the hermit lived. The arrow meant for the hind struck Giles instead. The king dismounted and expressed regret at the accident. He gave orders that the hind should not be hunted and, in private, the king returned several times to speak with Giles. The hermit urged the king to build a monastery in that place. The king said he would do so, provided Giles agreed to be its first Abbot.

Such a touching story prompted the dedication of many churches in the Middle Ages with the name of St. Giles, including the one at Stony Stratford. Actually Stony Stratford had two medieval churches. One of them, St. Mary Magdalene's, was virtually totally destroyed by fire in 1742. (Only the tower remained, and is still there.) Though money was raised to rebuild St. Mary Magdalene's, it was decided instead to refurbish St. Giles Church and to combine the two parishes in one. This was successfully accomplished. Today the Parish Church has a double dedication – St. Mary and St. Giles.

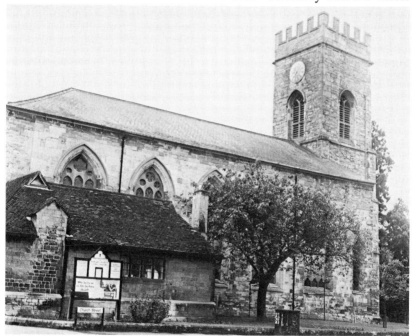

St. Giles, Stony Stratford, one of more than 150 churches dedicated to St. Giles, Patron Saint of Cripples and Beggars.

But the 'St. Mary' part of that title relates, not to the burnt down St. Mary Magdalene's, but to another (Victorian) St. Mary the Virgin's Church, which was built when the Wolverton Railway Works were being developed. That church was found not to be needed after all, so its congregation was merged with that of St. Giles in the now styled Parish Church of St. Mary and St. Giles, Stony Stratford. And the tiny little church in the fields at Tattenhoe is also St. Giles'. And so are the churches at Water Stratford and Cheddington.

Lawrence

Lawrence does pretty well in these parts. He scores eight churches locally. Five of them spell him with a 'w' (at Winslow, West Wycombe, Broughton, Bradwell and Cholesbury). The other three spell him with a 'u' (at Weston Underwood, Upton and Chicheley).

Altogether there are well over two hundred and forty St. Lawrence churches in England. So who was he? He was Archdeacon of Rome at a very tough time in the 3rd century. Persecution raged under the Emperor Valerian. Lawrence was one of the many to lose his life – in his case being burnt alive on a gridiron. (It is said that during the proceedings he said to his executioners: 'Turn me, I am done on this side!') The church in Broughton named in his honour is famous for some very fine medieval murals. Some of them depict lesser-known, not to say obscure saints.

Nicholas

Another saint who scores even better in these parts is *Nicholas*. Of over four hundred and thirty St. Nicholas Churches in England, thirteen are in Bucks. The nearest to Milton Keynes are at Little Horwood, Cublington and Lillingstone Dayrell.

Santa Claus is a contraction of the name Saint Nicholas, and in Germany he is regarded at the Patron Saint of children. His feast day is December 6th and it was a widespread custom on the continent each year on December 5th, the eve of his feast, for someone to assume the costume of a Bishop and to distribute gifts to 'good children'. A variation of this custom was introduced into this country from Germany in about 1840, and developed into the Christmas/Santa Claus tradition familiar to us all. (The factual background to St. Nicholas is that he was a 4th century Bishop of Myra in Lycia. He died in 326 AD.)

Swithun

'If it rains on *St. Swithun's* Day (15th July) there will be rain for forty days'. Who was St. Swithun? And how did that legend start?

Swithun was Bishop of Winchester and died in 862. He had asked to be buried in the Minster Churchyard so that 'the sweet rain of heaven might fall upon his grave'. He was buried in the churchyard as he had asked. But in the following century, when he had been declared a saint, the monks thought his remains should be moved into the Cathedral and buried there in the Choir. 15 July, 971 AD was the date fixed for this ceremony. And – you've guessed it – it poured with rain that day and for the next forty days as well. Are the parishioners at Swanborne good meteorologists? Their church is dedicated to St. Swithun.

Saints' names are frequently given to children at their baptism but Botolph is not likely to among them! St. Botolph was a 16th century Benedictine monk. All of our three counties have churches named after him – at Bradenham in Buckinghamshire, at Apsley Guise in Bedfordshire, and at Barton Seagrave and Church Brampton in Northamptonshire.

Ashby St. Ledger's church in Northamptonshire has the unusual dedication of the Blessed Virgin Mary and St. Leodegarious. That's another saint whose name is hardly likely to be given at the font, but he has given his name to one of the great classic races on the turf!

Assumption

Every saint has his or her special day each year in the calendar. Some saints have more than one day. And one of them has six. And that is *St. Mary the Virgin.*

It comes as no surprise that St. Mary's is the dedication of several thousand churches. But what is perhaps surprising is that so many churches with the dedication of St. Mary are in fact churches dedicated to the *Assumption* of the Blessed Virgin Mary. Her Assumption means that her earthly life was thought not to have ended by her death, but by her being taken or assumed into heaven. This is the doctrine of the Roman Catholic Church. It has never been endorsed formally as an Anglican doctrine. Yet of sixty Anglican churches in Buckinghamshire dedicated to St. Mary, no less than twelve are dedicated not just to her by name but to her Assumption into heaven. They are the churches at Beachampton, Wavendon, Woughton, Moulsoe, Leckampstead, Lillington Lovell, Stowe, Turweston, North Marston and Twyford.

All of these ancient churches were of course built and named long before the Reformation. They reflect the devotion of their founders and builders to the belief that so unique a person as the Blessed Virgin Mary 'fell asleep' rather than died and was assumed into heaven.

There could be a geographical explanation as well. When you mark the sites of all the churches of the Assumption of the BVM on a map, they appear to mark the routes of pilgrims to England's holiest shrine, that of Our Lady of Walsingham. In his little book, 'Church Dedications of the Oxford Diocese', Kenneth Kirk the former Bishop of Oxford developed this theme. He wrote: 'Of the 45 dedications of the Assumption in the country no less than 17 occur in the Oxford Diocese . . . ten all lie in a little strip of North Buckinghamshire about twenty miles long and eight miles broad, through the length of which runs the so-called Bedfordshire Ouse'. And he concludes: 'Thus the evidence points to Walsingham as the goal to which all the routes are directed'.

Other days – other customs. New churches are still being built as the city of Milton Keynes grows. Names have to be found for them too. It is interesting that one of them is the Cross and Stable Church. And of course the new City Centre Church is The Church of Christ The Cornerstone.

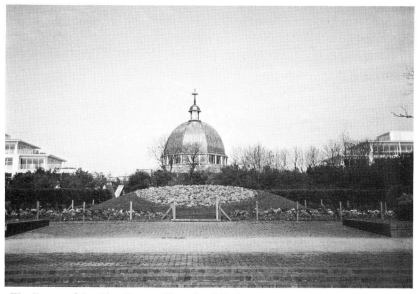

The Dome of the City Centre Church of Christ the Cornerstone in Milton Keynes. This ecumenical church is shared by Roman Catholics, Anglicans and Protestants.

Chapter 10

A PANORAMA OF PARSONS

A panorama is an overall view. In the foreground and middle distance – lots of detail; in the far distance the detail is obscure and only an outline of shape is suggested.

The same could be said of our panorama of parsons. Many a parish can trace the list of its parsons back to the 12th and 13th century. We can look at their names on the board at the back of the church and wonder about them. For most of us search in archives is not easy, but as we come nearer to our own times other sources of information are more readily available. There are references in history books, and sometimes in diaries, and quite often in Church Guides, many of which are excellent.

Sometimes, in a long list of rectors whose names mean nothing to us, we suddenly come across one about whom we know quite a lot. It is as if a column of men is passing by in the darkness, and then suddenly a spotlight comes on and picks out one of them. John Schorne, Vicar of North Marston is a good example. He was vicar there in the 13th century. (See page 54.)

The tiny parish of Milton Keynes provides other examples. Walter de Keynes wasn't its first parson, but we know he was Rector in about 1291 and probably built the chancel of the church. But there followed him some seventeen parsons about whom we only know their names. Then, in 1559, there came Francis Babbington. He was Rector of Lincoln College, Oxford, Rector of Milton Keynes and also of Adstock. We do know a little more about him because, being a Roman Catholic, and not willing to become otherwise, he had to flee overseas to save his life.

Four incumbents later we come to a Rector who is much more than just a name. He was the Reverend Lewis Atterbury. Two things make his name familiar. The first is that he died in tragic circumstances. He fell off his horse and was drowned in 1693 while riding back from London to Milton Keynes. The accident happened as he was passing the bridge at Newport Pagnell during a great flood.

The second reason we know about him is because he had a son, born in the Rectory at Milton Keynes, who became famous, or as some would have said, infamous. He was the Reverend Francis Atterbury. He was educated at Westminster, and did brilliantly at Christ Church, Oxford. After ordination he became the leading preacher and controversialist of the High Church and Tory Party. He became in turn Dean of Carlisle, Bishop of Rochester, and Dean of Westminster. He was a great orator and debater in the House of Lords. He officiated at the coronation of George I, but it was known that his sympathies lay with the Stuarts.

In 1720 he was arrested and accused of plotting with the Jacobites. Stripped of all his ecclesiastical appointments, he was banished from England in 1723. He died in exile in France in 1732, but in a way he had the last word – his body was brought back to England and privately buried in Westminster Abbey.

In 1693 the Rector of Milton Keynes was the Rev. Dr William Wotten, a man of prodigious knowledge and authorship. He took in as guest and pupil the young Browne Willis, and imparted to him his enthusiasm for antiquarian studies. (See page 62.)

The Bletchley Diarist
Of one local parson in the 18th century we know a very great deal. For he was the Reverend William Cole, the Rector of St. Mary's, Bletchley, and a famous diarist. He was Rector of Bletchley from 1753 to 1767. Here are a couple of revealing extracts from his diary:

'The Clark, Wm Wood had been drunk for a week together and was so drunk this morning that I was sent to, to desire that Will Turpin might officiate as Clark, he being sexton. I was sorry to do this as he, Wm Wood, is a quiet good-tempered Man, and no fault but drunkenness. He had not lain at my house these 2 or 3 nights, but at an Ale House at Fenny Stratford, the Sink of all that is bad'.

❖ ❖ ❖ ❖ ❖

'I receive a Citation from the Rt. Rev. John Green, Bp. of Lincoln . . . to attend his Visitation at Newport Pagnell on the 27th following, when I am to pay my Procurations, exhibit my Letters of Orders, and he is to confirm the Children of my Parish, when there is barely 3 weeks Notice to prepare them for that Ordinance. And when he comes, it is done in such a hurry, with such noise and confusion, as to seem more like a Bear Baiting than any Religious Institution, and must haste to have it over, that it evidently appears that it is no small Burthen to attend at all, that such Farces make one ashamed and confused'.

Keach of Winslow
From 1660 to 1668 Benjamin Keach was Pastor of the tiny Baptist church in Winslow. Those were days of religious intolerance when dissenting ministers were often persecuted. Keach was arrested both because of his preaching and his writing. His spoken and written words were deemed to be 'to the great displeasure of God and the King's peace'. He was fined £20, sent to prison for two weeks, and, as our cover picture shows, he was made to stand in the pillory at Aylesbury and also at Winslow. In both places Keach used the pillory as a pulpit, preaching to the onlookers.

Now meet a very strange figure in our panorama of parsons. He is Richard Carpenter (1609–1670). Was he a parson? If so, what sort?

Richard Carpenter was a Roman Catholic, born in Newport Pagnell. He made his way to Rome. There he was commissioned by the Pope to return to England as a Benedictine to work for England's conversion. But something went wrong, and Carpenter became an Anglican. Later, he changed again, and became an Independent Minister.

Having left the C of E, he attacked it vigorously. He also roundly abused the Baptists, against whom he wrote a pamphlet which he entitled:

'*ANABAPTISTS WASHT AND WASHT AND SHRUNK IN THE WASHING*'.

He preached at Aylesbury with some effect. He returned finally into the Roman fold.

Enter the Wesleys

In the 18th century the Church of England was badly in need of a shake up. At Oxford University in 1729 a group of pious Anglican students tried to do something about it. They formed

This pulpit in Upper Winchendon Church was made from one solid piece of oak. John Wesley preached his first sermon from it after his ordination in Oxford in 1725.

The Wesley Elm, Stony Stratford. John Wesley preached here three times, but he found Stony a hard nut to crack.

The Holy Club, concentrating on worship combined with works of charity. The leaders were John and Charles Wesley.

The Holy Club only lasted till 1735, but its influence continued through the ministry of the two Wesley brothers, both of whom were ordained in the Anglican ministry. The name 'Methodist' was coined because John Wesley urged that Christians should live according to the method of life given in the Scriptures. This is the origin of what became the Methodist denomination, separate from the Church of England. But John and Charles Wesley remained priests in the Church of England until they died. They still hoped to wake up the established church from the inside, but were frustrated by the opposition of the bishops and many of the clergy. They took to travelling extensively all over the country, preaching to large crowds – in the open air because they were denied access to church pulpits.

That programme of itinerant preaching brought John Wesley three times to Stony Stratford. His first visit was on

July 30th, 1777. By then he was in his seventies, but still vigorous. He recorded his visit in his diary: 'Mr Canham had prepared a large and commodious place, but it would not contain the congregation. However, all without, as well as within, except one fine lady, were serious and attentative'. One wonders what the fine lady had done to be singled out.

Four months later he was back in Stony Stratford again. This time his diary gives just a little hint that he found Stony a hard nut to crack: 'At Stony Stratford. Congregation large and attentative as it always is. Yet I fear they received little good for *"they need no repentence"'.*

Two years later, in 1779, came a third visit. By now he was seventy-six. The visit prompted only the briefest entry in his diary: 'Preached at Stony Stratford'. At his first visit he had preached under what became known as 'Wesley's Elm' on the Market Square. The two later sermons were preached in a large barn behind the old Talbot Inn.

'Daddy' Guest

Not every parson gets to have a pub named after him. It happened to the Reverend Newman Guest. There are many who still remember him, for he was truly an eccentric man. He was Vicar of St. James Church, New Bradwell, from well before World War I right up to the years of World War II. (1909–1946). He invariably wore an old pair of what he would have called plimsolls (trainers), and could be seen frequently riding his bicycle, with his feet up on either side of the front mudguard when he coasted downhill.

This remarkable Irishman was appointed Vicar of New Bradwell in 1909. His church, St. James, was a Victorian building, erected in 1860 to meet the needs of the workers in Wolverton Railway Works. Like St. George's Church in Wolverton, the building had been provided by the London and Northwestern Railway. Ecclesiastically, it took the place of the ancient parish church at Stanton Low, about a mile away. (A Norman arch from the old Stanton Low Church has been built into the west wall of St. James' Church.)

93

The Victorian church of St. James, New Bradwell, has a Norman arch from the ancient church of Stanton Low at its west end. The Vicar caused a sensation in 1909 when he said that more than 400 weddings solemnised there had been invalid.

Nobody had thought, in 1860, to make sure that the new church was properly licensed for marriages. It was just assumed automatically that the pastoral responsibilities of the old parish church at Stanton Low had devolved on the new parish, including the administration of the sacrament of Holy Matrimony. Unfortunately, and technically, this was not so. This awful realisation surfaced soon after the new Vicar was appointed. A frantic examination of the church registers revealed that between 1860 and 1909 a total of 434 marriages had been solemnised at St. James' Church. In the eyes of the church all these couples had been properly wed. In the eyes of the State they had not.

Never one to waste a good opportunity to 'make a drama out of a crisis', the Reverend Newman Guest astonished his congregation at Evensong one March evening in 1909 by telling them that more than eight hundred people, married in St. James' Church up to that time, had not, in one sense, been married at all! So they had all been living in sin! And all their offspring were therefore illegitimate! Sensation – embarrassment – anger! The Vicar hastened to add that action would be taken to put matters right.

The appropriate action was taken – by the Home Secretary. The Government passed a Provisional Order in Council declaring retroactively that all those previous marriages could be regarded as valid, and all the offspring resulting from them were thereby legitimised.

In the air-raids of World War II Wolverton and its surroundings would have constituted a 'legitimate' target. Yet despite many Air Raid Warnings, the area escaped almost scot-free. Almost – but not quite. One bomb did some slight damage to 'Daddy Guest's' Church of St. James. But nobody suggested it was belated divine retribution for all those early dodgy weddings!

Daddy Guest has long since gone to his reward. He certainly left many memories behind him, and a pub, The Jovial Priest in Bradville serves as a kind of memorial to him. So too did a play all about him produced some years ago in Stantonbury Theatre.

In this panorama of parsons there are several who rate a special mention for sheer length of service. The little parish of Moulsoe provides a good example.

Long Service Medals
Nicholas Bloddington was presented to the Parish of Moulsoe as Rector in 1223 by the Prioress of Goring. David Morgan-Evans was presented to the Parish of Moulsoe as Rector in 1938 by Lord Carrington, father of the former Foreign Secretary. He retired in 1985 but Lord Carrington said that he could continue to live at the Rectory. He died there in 1992, aged ninety-three.

His official tenure as Rector, therefore, was forty-seven years, from 1938 to 1985. In his last years as Rector he had the distinction of being the oldest serving clergyman in the Church of England.

You might suppose that in the long line of Rectors of Moulsoe, from Nicholas Bloddington to Morgan-Evans the latter's tenure would be the longest. Not so. His '47 not out' is handsomely exceeded by Richard Cautley, who put in no less than fifty-six years as Rector before dying on February 28th 1842. Cautley's widow, Octavia, survived him for thirty-one years, dying in 1873 aged ninety-five years. There was no widow of Morgan-Evans to challenge Octavia, for Morgan-Evans was a bachelor. He died on 2nd November 1992.

David Morgan-Evans was ordained priest in 1930, so he celebrated his Golden Jubilee in 1980 and his Diamond Jubilee in 1990. The first nine years in the ministry he spent as curate in the parish of Llanryst in St. David's Diocese. His duties there included the Chaplaincy at Gwydyr Castle, seat of the Marquess of Lincolnshire. So it came about that when Lord Carrington, kinsman of the Marquess, needed a Rector for Moulsoe, the young Welsh Curate was invited to London to be interviewed. The interview was to be at Lord Carrington's Club. Getting there was a bit daunting for Morgan whose courage finally failed him in a London taxi. He suddenly panicked at the thought that the cabby might be taking him absolutely *anywhere.* So, when the taxi halted at some traffic lights, he ducked out of it and legged it into Green Park. The taxi driver's feelings on losing both his client and his fare are not known, but easily imagined. 'And him a parson too!'

Moulsoe, now in Newport Pagnell Deanery, is only in Oxford Diocese by a whisker. Its population is about three hundred, its church basically 13th century with alterations, its Rectory Georgian and enormous. The parish has not been spared the changes common to most villages. The days of fifteen in the choir and sixty plus at Evensong every week are gone. So many other changes too. Morgan-Evans commented: 'There used to be just three cars in the village, mine and two others. Now there are about two hundred'.

If you've been Rector of a small village for nearly half a century you can be forgiven if you sometimes indulge in nostalgia. 'You see that two-acre paddock just beyond the lawn

– I used to put that down to potatoes, and I loved to be out there working at five in the morning. First you'd hear the cuckoo, then the school bell, and then the sound of the hammer on the anvil at the smithy'. There are no potatoes planted now – no school bell, and no smithy, but the cuckoo can still be heard in that lovely countryside on the northern edges of Buckinghamshire, looking across to the Brickhills. And David Morgan-Evans, in his nineties, looked back across the length of years.

Little more than ten miles from Moulsoe is the Parish of Emberton. It once had a Rector who served there even longer than Morgan-Evans did at Moulsoe. He was the Reverend Thomas Fry who became Rector of Emberton in 1804 and served the parish for almost sixty years. A clock tower in the village is his memorial to his wife Margaret.

The Parish of St. James, Great Horwood can boast a 'half-centenarian' Rector. He was the Reverend Simon Thomas Adams, born 1807, died 1889. Of the eighty-two years of his life exactly fifty were spent as Rector of Great Horwood, 1839–1889.

The Parish of St. George, Wolverton can claim no 'Half-centenarian' incumbent, but it has its own claim to distinction in that for almost exactly three-quarters of a century two priests, father and son, served as Vicar. First came Francis William Harnett, vicar from 1860 to 1894. He was succeeded by his son, William Lee Harnett, vicar from 1894 to 1934.

Things are ordered differently nowadays. Parsons move, or are moved, much more frequently. The days of a parson's freehold are over. It is no longer the case that an incumbent, appointed to a parish, can stay there for as long as he wishes. His appointment will nowadays be for a set number of years. But one aspect of the parson's job does remain unchanged. He continues to be a parson even if he doesn't stay for years in one parish. And he is still a parson even when he retires. 'Thou art a priest for ever after the order of Melchisedec'.

Chapter 11

THE WILLEN STORY

No part of Milton Keynes has a more fascinating story than Willen. It was included in Domesday Book, bracketed as a manor with Caldecot. It has been variously spelt. Wyllyne is one version; Welyn-cum-Caldecot is another. After the Conquest the Church of Wylene (yet another spelling) was given to the Priory of Tickford. Early in the 13th century lands in Willene (a fourth spelling!) were given to Snelshall Priory.

These two very early monastic connections were to have an interesting post-script some seven hundred years later, as we shall see.

There has been a church at Willen for at least eight hundred years though the present building dates only from 1680. The list of Vicars is complete, right back to Alanus who was the incumbent in 1223.

It was always a very small village. By the time of the 1841 Census its population had risen to ninety-seven, but even in 1973 the village proper comprised only seventeen households.

The Manor changed hands many times over the centuries. In the 17th century, during the Civil War, it belonged to Robert Hammond, a Colonel in Cromwell's Parliamentary Army. He was the man put in charge of King Charles I after his defeat in the Civil War. When Charles I was captured he was held under house arrest for the first few days at Woburn and later at Holdenby, where part of the garden is still called King Charles's Walk. Eventually he was sent to the Isle of Wight where Colonel Hammond, the Governor of the Isle of Wight, became his warder.

Willen Church – 'a city church that unaccountably strayed into the country'?

When Hammond died he left no male heir, only three young daughters. So, by an Act of Parliament of 1673, the estate passed to the Reverend Dr Richard Busby, Prebendary of Westminster Abbey, and a celebrated Headmaster of Westminster School. He came to live in Willen, and his coming had a profound effect on the place.

It was Dr Busby who built the present church in 1680. Or, rather, he commissioned Robert Hooke to design and build it. Hooke had been a friend and collaborator of Christopher Wren, and both of them had been Dr Busby's pupils at Westminster School.

*Grinling Gibbon's Font
Cover in Willen Church.
He excelled in the wood
carving of fruit and
flowers.*

Following the disastrous Great Fire of London in 1666 Wren
and his associates had built so many new churches in London.
Now Hooke was commissioned to build a church for Willen in
1680. So perhaps the following comment by John Camp in his
'Portrait of Buckinghamshire' is rather apt. He writes:

> *'Willen Church is odd, not because of its ugliness but
> rather the reverse. It looks in fact a little alien in its
> surroundings, as if a city church had unaccountably
> strayed into the country and decided to remain. And this,
> in a way, is rather what has happened. Willen Church
> was built in 1680 by Robert Hooke in the style and
> manner of the city churches of Christopher Wren, his
> friend and collaborator.'*

Camp goes on to praise the church, speaking of its design as
'pure italian', and of the fine plaster ceiling as 'an astonishing
work of art'. Part of the charm of this little church is that

everything in it is consistent with everything else. All the pews, the pulpit, the organ case and other furnishings are contemporary with the church itself. The font cover is by Grinling Gibbons, the celebrated Dutch-born British sculptor. Gibbons excelled in the carving of fruit and flowers in wood. From Christopher Wren he had the commission to work on the choir stalls and organ screen of the new St. Paul's Cathedral, and from Hooke he had the commission to make the delightful font cover for Willen Church.

A special feature of Dr Busby's creation of the new church at Willen was his gift of a Library. At one stage it comprised 620 leather-bound volumes of 16th, 17th and 18th century authorship, chiefly theological works. Most were the gift of Dr Busby, and others were added later by Hume, the Rector of Bradwell. Initially the Library was housed in 'the North Chamber adjoining the tower' of St. Mary Magdalene's Church, but later it was moved to the Vicarage. Just as the early monastic connections of Willen Church were to have an interesting postscript seven hundred years later, so too this 17th century Library was to have an interesting postscript some three centuries later.

In the nineteen-forties the Vicarage was burned down and a new Vicarage was built. But the days of a Vicar exclusively for Willen were about to end. As the new city of Milton Keynes came into being, the Bishop of Oxford invited an Anglican Religious Order, the Society of the Sacred Mission, to open a Priory at Willen.

The Mother House of SSM had been at Kelham, near Newark Upon Trent. One of its principal works there had been the training of theological students for the ministry. But a rationalisation of Anglican theological colleges led to the closing of some and the merging of others. In that process Kelham closed down, and so some of the members of the Community were free to accept the Bishop's invitation to open a small Priory at Willen. The newly-built Vicarage became the nucleus of the new Priory buildings, and the Church, while still the place of worship for the locality, could also be used by the members of the Community.

So it came about that seven hundred years after its former links with Tickford Priory and Snelshall Priory, Willen again had a link with a Religious Community.

One unusual and dramatic link between Willen Priory and the Kelham Mother House from which it came, is the very striking Jagger Calvary which stands today in the Priory garden at Willen. At Kelham this fine Calvary had stood on a huge arch in the Chapel used by the theological students and the members of the Community.

Part of the thinking behind the invitation to open a Priory at Willen was that it would give the new city of Milton Keynes a spiritual resource centre – a place for conference and retreat. The Brethren of the Priory, corporately, acted as the Incumbent of the Parish of Willen. This arrangement lasted for about a decade. Then, as Milton Keynes developed, Willen Parish became part of the Ecumenical Parish of Stantonbury. One of the Team of seven full-time ministers in that huge parish is Team Vicar of Willen. The Priory continues to use Willen Church three times every day.

At the Priory there is a good Library and Resource Centre for teachers, parents and clergy. So the 17th century Library of Dr Busby has its 20th century counterpart today.

The name Willen took on a new dimension of enormous importance in 1974. In that year Willen Hospice of Our Lady and St. John began its work. Initially it was the inspiration of Lady Marjorie Reid. She was a Doctor who saw the need for such a Hospice.

Where should it be sited? How could it be financed? Providentially, hard by Willen Church, on the shores of Willen Lake there stood a fine old farm house. Could that be the nucleus of the Hospice? Yes, it could. And it had another virtue too. Lady Reid believed strongly that the Hospice should if possible be associated with a Religious Community. And there, on the spot, was the Priory of the SSM.

By 1979 the dream had begun to become a reality and the first patients were accepted. Little by little the site has been developed, and today the Hospice is a place of tranquility and

The Jagger Calvary in Willen Priory Garden

calm on the shores of a lake which is a Bird Sanctuary and Nature Reserve. It is called the Hospice of Our Lady and St. John, and appropriately in the nearby Priory garden stands that Jagger Calvary, with the strong figures of Our Lady and St. John standing at the foot of the cross.

So many people have helped to make all this possible. But Marjorie Reid will always be remembered as the one who had the vision to see what was needed, the determination to overcome all the difficulties, and the faith to persevere till the dream became a reality. As it happened, she herself fell ill in late 1990 and died from the very illness she had helped so many other to bear. A colleague, writing of her death, said: 'She died as she hoped the Hospice would help others to die, in peace and faith'.

THE ROYALTIES FROM THIS BOOK ALL GO TO THE SUPPORT OF THE WILLEN HOSPICE OF OUR LADY AND ST. JOHN.

Willen Hospice – a haven of peace and tranquility.

Monks have featured in the Willen story several times already – pre-reformation Catholic monks in the 12th century, and Anglican monks in the 20th century. But recent years have brought monks of a quite different sort too – Buddhist monks. They came to Willen in the seventies and numbered a dozen or more. Their shaven heads and bright yellow saffron robes became a familiar sight. They were here for a very special purpose – to construct the Peace Pagoda which overlooks Willen Lake. There are several such Peace Pagodas elsewhere in the world. The Willen Pagoda was the first to be erected in the west. In huge bas-relief marble panels the Pagoda tells the story of the life of Buddha, born 2,500 years ago.

When the huge Pagoda was finished in 1980 the opening ceremony to mark the occasion was an astonishing affair. Dignatories from all over the world were present, and richly caparisoned elephants featured in the procession. In the rich tapestry of the Willen story over many centuries, the Buddhist presence and the Pagoda they created are surely among the most colourful threads.

One final aspect completes the Willen story. It concerns the lake. Willen Lake is almost two lakes. The smaller portion is the one overlooked by Willen Hospice. It is a Bird Sanctuary. Its peace and tranquility, and the wide variety of bird life it attracts are a therapeutic bonus for patients and staff at the Hospice.

The larger part of Willen Lake is almost certainly the most popular resort in Milton Keynes for family enjoyment. As well as all the water sports that can be enjoyed there, the extensive area around the lake offers a wide range of amenities and attractions. There is an Adventure Playground, a 'bowl' arena, a maze, and a number of play areas. All in all, Willen Lake gives pleasure to every age group.

The tiny hamlet of Willen, with its fascinating history, and with all its varied contributions to the life of the community, now takes its place in the larger setting of the expanding city of Milton Keynes – and a very worthy place too.

Chapter 12

THREE CHEERS FOR BOW BRICKHILL

Cheer No. 1

All Saints, Bow Brickhill is probably the only church in North Bucks. to be the subject of a famous painting in a London Gallery.

The painting by Thomas Webster was commissioned in 1847 by Mr John Sheepshanks, and was exhibited that year in the Royal Academy. Its title is 'The Village Choir' and it shows the old west gallery of the church, with twenty-two men, women and children singing in the choir.

'The Village Choir' hangs in the Victoria and Albert Museum.

All of them were instantly recognisable, and all of them lived in the village. Three of them are seen playing instruments, bassoon, clarionet and ' cello.

In 1857 Mr Sheepshanks bequeathed the painting to the Victoria and Albert Museum, where it still hangs.

Descendants of those figured in the painting are able to identify their relatives, and in some instances still possess such items as silk neckerchiefs seen in the picture.

Cheer No. 2
All Saints, Bow Brickhill was the first church in North Buckinghamshire known to have had a hymn-tune named after it. The tune, 'Bow Brickhill', was composed by Sir Sydney Nicholson and is sung to the hymn:

'We sing the praise of Him who died'.

Wavendon now enjoys a similar distinction. A hymn tune composed by John Dankworth is called Wavendon.

Cheer No. 3
Bow Brickhill Church was the first Parish church in all England to affiliate to the School of English Church Music. It was Sir Sydney Nicholson, Organist and Master of Choristers at Westminster Abbey, who founded the School of English Church Music in 1927.

Sir Sydney Nicholson lived in Bow Brickhill, and for a number of years the boy choristers from Westminster Abbey used to come in the summer months to camp at Bow Brickhill. They slept in old railway carriages parked on the south side of the hill. Long afterwards people recalled with pleasure their singing round the campfire in the evening.

In 1987, when the School of English Church Music celebrated its Diamond Jubilee, the BBC marked the occasion by broadcasting 'Songs of Praise' from All Saints Church. Former Westminster Abbey choristers joined Bow Brickhill choristers in the service. And of course Sir Sydney Nicholson's hymn featured in the service.

But some earlier chapters in the history of Bow Brickhill Church had been less happy. A church has existed in the village since the 12th century, always on that magnificent site on the side of the hill.

In the 17th century it passed through trying times. During the Civil War a Roundhead Army held Brickhill Ridge and used the towers of all three Brickhill churches for look-out posts.

All Saints Church soon after that fell into disrepair and was virtually unused and unusable for a century and a half. That sad chapter came happily to an end in 1756 when Browne Willis gave or found the money to save the church and to put it back into good repair.

All Saints, Bow Brickhill. Its tower was a Telegraph Station in the war against Napoleon, and was used by the Royal Observer Corps in the war against Hitler.

Chapter 13

'TO SEE A FINE LADY . . .'

'Ride a cock horse
to Banbury Cross
to see a fine lady
upon a white horse'

Was Celia Fiennes that fine lady? Maybe. She certainly rode a horse and several times went to Banbury. Her name, Fiennes, is pronounced 'fines' and Celia was certainly a Lady by birth and family connections. She was the granddaughter of William Fiennes, 8th Baron and 1st Viscount Saye and Sele of Broughton Castle. *'to see a Fiennes Lady upon a white horse?'* was probably the original version.

William Fiennes of Broughton Castle married Elizabeth Temple of Stowe. Their granddaughter, Celia, was born in 1662. She never married and at about the age of twenty she began those incredible journeys on horseback which took her into every county in England. She rode side-saddle of course, and without any great retinue – just a couple of servants at most, and she covered immense distances. Her journeys took her from the Isle of Wight to Yorkshire, from Penzance to Newcastle, from London to Carlisle. *And* she kept a diary.

She claimed that her journeys were undertaken to regain her health, and that her Diary was not intended for publication, but only for the interest of her near relations. This can hardly be true, though, because she herself in a Preface to it, wrote: 'I shall conclude with a hearty wish and recommendation to all, but especially my own Sex, the studdy of those things which tends to improve the mind and makes our Lives pleasant and comfortable as well as profitable in all the Stages and Stations of our Lives, and render Suffering and Age supportable and Death less formidable and a future State more happy.'

It was not until 1888 that a short version of her diary reached a wider public, entitled: *'Through England on a side saddle in the time of William and Mary'*. This small edition was followed in 1947 by a much fuller, annotated, version: *'The Illustrated Journeys of Celia Fiennes, 1685–c1712'*, edited by Christopher Morris. Christopher Morris had worked at Bletchley Park in World War II on German naval ciphers and went on to teach history at King's College, Cambridge. His book is the definitive work on Celia's Journeys and Diary.

With all her family connections Celia did not lack for places to visit or for kinsfolk with whom to stay. Her grandfather had married a Temple of Stowe, his half-sister married a Villiers, and his oldest son married a Cecil. Celia's aunts were married respectively to one peer, two baronets, a baronet's son, and the son of a knight. On her mother's side, too, Celia had plenty of kinsfolk to visit, many of them country squires, while others were prominent in Law or in business.

Aylesbury, Bedford, Buckingham, Dunstable, St. Albans, Stony Stratford, Woburn, Great Horwood, Thornton and Stowe – all figured in Celia's journeys and therefore in her Diary. It is fascinating to imagine this intrepid lady riding on horseback, virtually alone, through our countryside nearly three hundred years ago – observing, commenting, and committing her thoughts to her Diary pages.

Celia's spelling and punctuation were often peculiar, and she could make factual mistakes too, as when she confused the Bedford Ouse which flows into the Wash with the Yorkshire Ouse. But none of this detracts from the interest of her Diary for us who read it three centuries later.

'Another journey from London to Alsebury (Aylesbury), from thence to great Horrwood; from thence I went to Hillsdon (Hillesden) a house of Mr Dentons which stands in the middle of a fine Parke; we went to Thorndon (Thornton) Sir Thomas Tyrrells, a good old house and very good gardens, some walks like arbours close . . . thence we went to Stowe, Sir Richard Temples new House that stands pretty high; you enter into a hall very lofty with a gallery round the top, thence through to a great parlour that opens in a ballcony to the garden, and is a vista thro' the whole house, so that on the one side you view the gardens which are one below another . . . replenished with all the curiosytes or requisites for ornament pleasure or use.'

'We went to Horrwood by severall other seates of Sir Ralph Verneys who has most exact fine gardens.' (Middle and East Claydon.)

'Within two mile off Horrwood is a well of minerall waters from iron just like Tunbridge and as good. I drank them a fortnight. There are severall of the same sort of springs all about that country.' (Celia stayed with her cousin Elizabeth who was married to Hugh Barker of Great Horwood.)

'Thence I went to Buckingham town, a very neate town and we passed the river Ouise over a very high bridge, tho' the river seemed not then so very full, but it swells after great raines, which makes them build their arches so large.'

(On a subsequent journey:) 'Thence to great Horwood, this country is fruitful, full of woods enclosures and rich ground, the little towns stand pretty thicke, you have many in view as you pass the road to Horwood. Thence we pass by a lofty pile of building called Salden a Gentlemans house; and by the rich Mrs Bennets house remarkable for covetousness which was the cause of her death, her treasures tempted a Butcher to cut her throate, who hangs in chaines just against her house. (See page 14.)

'Thence to Ouburn (Woburn) the Duke of Bedford's house we saw, which stands in a fine parke full of deer and wood, and some off the trees are kept cut in works and the shape of severall beasts; the gardens are fine, there is a large bowling green with 8 arbours kept neately, and seates in each. There are 3 large gardens full of fruite – I eate a great quantety of the Red Coralina goosbery, which is a large, thin skin'd sweete goosebery . . . In a Cherry Garden in the midst stands a figure of stone resembling an old weeder woman used in the garden and my Lord would have her Effigie which is done so like and her clothes so well that first I tooke it to be a real living body.'

'From thence we came to Dunstable over a sad road called Hockley in the Hole (Hockliffe) as full of deep slows (sloughs) in the winter it must be impasable, there is a very good pitch's Causey for foote people and horses that is raised up high from the Roade, and a very steep chaulky hill whence it has its name the Chalk Hill just as you enter Dunstable. Its a good town as you shall meete with on the Road, its full of Inns, there is a long large streete with a great water in the streete it looks like a large pond.'

'Thence to St. Albans; there is a very large streete to the Market Place; its a pretty large towne takeing all, the St. Juliers and that at one end, and the other end is St. Nicholas where is a handsome Church. The great Church which is dedicated to St. Albans is much out of repaire; I see the places in the pavement that was worn like holes for kneeling by the devotes of the Religion, and his votereys as they tell you, but the whole Church is so worn away that it mourns for some charitable person to help repaire it.'

'To Stony Stratford so cross the river Aven (Ouse) again; Stony Stratford is a little place built all stone; they make a great deale of Bonelace and so they do all hereabout, its the manuffactory of this part of the country, they sit and worke all along the streete as thick as can be.'

'Thence to Bedford town. Bedford town is an old building its washed by the river Ouse which is here broader than in most places till it reaches Yorke, its stored with very good fish, and those which have gardens on its brinke keeps sort of trunck or what they call them – its a receptacle of wood of a pretty size full of holes to let the water in and out – here they keep fish they catch as pike perch tench etc, so they have it readye for their use. This is of mighty advantage especially for the Publick houses, you see the fish taken out fresh for supper or dinner; the river runns twineing about and runns into severall notches of ground which is sett full of willows, and many little boates chained to the side belonging to the people of the town for their diversion; it runns by a ground which is made into a fine bowling-green; its upon a hill and a pretty ascent from the river that is besett with willows all round beneath; the bowling-green is well kept with seates and summer houses in it for the use of the Town and Country Gentlemen of which many resort to it especially the Market dayes; at the entrance of the town you pass over the river on a bridge which has a gate on it and some houses. The Market House is on severall stone pillars and raill'd in; there is above it roomes which were design'd for the session and publick buissness of the town by the Lord Russell that built it, but his untimely death, being beheaded, put a stop to its finishing; they now put it to noe use but spinning, haveing begun to sett up the woolen worke; but its just in its infancy.' (Lord William Russell had been executed in 1683 following the Rye House Plot.)

'I went to Laighton Buserd (Leighton Buzzard) and thence to Whinslow (Winslow); thence to Broughton and staid a weeke and then returned through Oxfford Citty and so to London.'

'To Northampton town which opens a noble prospect to your sight a mile distant, a large town well built, the streetes as large as most in London except Holborn and the Strand, the houses well built of brick and stone – some all stone – very regular buildings; the Town Hall is new built all stone and resembles the Guildhall in little; the Church is new built its very neate; there is two rows of stone pillars at the entrance of the Church on the outside; there is abundance of new buildings which adds to the beauty of the town.'

'I went to Asply (Aspley Guise) where the earth turns wood into stone and had a piece of it, it seemes its only one sort of wood the Aldertree which turns so, and lay or drive a paille or stake into the ground there, in seven years its petrify'd into stone.'

Celia's journeys through the English countryside were not without danger. Her Diary records one unpleasant incident: 'Here I think I may say was the only tyme I had reason to suspect I was engaged with some Highway men; 2 fellows all

300 years ago Celia Fiennes described Northampton Parish Church as 'new built, very neate'. Here the Oakapple ceremony takes place every May 29th.

on a suddain from the wood fell into the road, they look';d truss'd up with great coates and as it were bundles about them which I believe was pistolls but they dogg'd me, one before, the other behind, and would often look back to each other and frequently justle my horse out of the way to get between one of my servants horses and mine, and when they first came up to us did disown their knowledge of the way and would often stay a little behind and talke together then come up againe, but the Providence of God so order'd it as there was men at work in the field hay makeing, and it being market day at Whitchurch as I drew near to that town in 3 or 4 mile was continually met with some of the market people.'

Three hundred years after the redoubtable Celia Fiennes made her impressive journeys throughout England, a kinsman of hers, Ranulph Fiennes, in the late twentieth century, was to make the news with journeys still more epic and hazardous – journeys to both North and South Poles.

Though Celia said she undertook her journeys to regain her health, she seems to have stayed remarkably fit. Everywhere she went she made a great thing of drinking the water of mineral wells and springs. She called them Spaws (Spas) and believed some of them to be 'diuretick', some to be 'quick purgers', and others to be 'good for all scurbutick humours'. She not only drank the Great Horwood waters for a fortnight, but also went annually for several years to take the waters at Tunbridge Wells.

She died in 1741, aged 79, while staying with one of her nieces at Hackney. She has left us all in her debt for the down-to-earth snapshots she left us of how life was three hundred years ago as she travelled:

'through England on a side saddle in the time of William and Mary'.

Chapter 14

MONOPOLY MONEY, AND THE GREAT TRAIN ROBBERY

Seventy men in Glasgow boarded the train late one August night in 1963. They were not passengers – for them a night's work was about to begin. While the train sped southwards towards London they would be sorting the mail.

Fifteen other men, of whom they knew nothing, were preparing a violent and unwelcome reception for them far to the south.

The overnight Mail Train from Glasgow to London carried surplus money from the banks, not only from Scotland, but also from other major towns the train passed through on the way south. The last pick-up was at Rugby.

The train comprised many coaches, but one of these was more important than the rest. It was the one known as the HVP coach – the High Value Package coach. This was always the second coach behind the locomotive. Working in it were five Post Office workers. The rest of the seventy were in the other coaches further back.

On a normal night's run the HVP coach would be carrying sixty or seventy mail bags by the time it left Rugby. But this was two days after the August Bank Holiday, so there would be up to two hundred and fifty bags aboard the HVP coach.

All this was known to the fifteen men waiting for that train. Months of preparation had gone into their plot, and everything had been thoroughly researched. Their hope was that the train would be carrying up to five million pounds in used bank notes.

There could be no hope of them robbing the train when it reached Euston, or at any of the stations through which it passed. The train must be stopped and robbed somewhere *between* the stations. But where? They needed a spot where a road bridge crossed the rail, with no nearby houses, and where the roads in the area were quiet and traffic-free.

Patient search had shown them just such a place. It was Bridge No. 127, Bridego Bridge, just a mile or two south of Linslade. The nearest house was a quarter of a mile away, Linslade and Leighton Buzzard a few miles to the north, and Mentmore Park, still then the stately home of Lord Rosebery, a mile away.

The group of fifteen was a strange mixture. It comprised two rival gangs. One of these had originated the idea of the robbery, but needed the expertise of the second gang to carry it out. That second gang was expert at halting trains – it had carried out some train robberies of its own on the Brighton

Bridego Bridge, near Linslade, where the Great Train Robbers stole £2,600,000.

Line. So the two gangs had agreed to combine.

But both gangs needed finance to set up this new project. They needed money to support the gang members during the months while the preparations were being made, and for the purchase of the several vehicles they would need. They also needed cash for the purchase of a hide-out where they could assemble both before and after the raid on the train.

The necessary finance came from a surprising source – from Germany. It amounted to £80,000, but the underground German investors exacted a high price for it. They advanced the money only on the understanding that they would get two million pounds out of the five million the raid on the train was expected to yield. Reluctantly the British villains agreed. After all, it would still leave something over £90,000 for each of them.

The choice of a suitable hide-out was crucial. They needed somewhere quiet and unobtrusive, where men and vehicles could be accommodated out of sight for two or three days before the robbery, and where the gang could lie low for at least three days after the raid on the train had taken place. They would need that time for the mammoth task of counting the money and sharing it out!

But there was another motive for planning to lie low after the raid. They reasoned that the Police would assume that the robbers would leave the scene of the crime immediately by the quickest route – along the M1 either to Birmingham or London.

They found exactly what they wanted. A small property called Leatherslade Farm, near Brill, was on the market. It was exactly right. The secluded farmhouse was down a quiet lane half a mile from its nearest neighbour. It had suitable outbuildings where their vehicles could be prepared under cover. Two of the vehicles they acquired were landrovers. The plan was to paint these to pass muster as military vehicles, and to repaint them immediately after the raid.

The purchase of Leatherslade Farm was achieved through an intermediary. Supplies were assembled there – ample food, cooking utensils, walkie-talkie radios, etc. And somebody added a Monopoly set!

From Leatherslade Farm to Bridego Bridge is about twenty-seven miles. They worked out a route from one to the other across the Vale of Aylesbury, avoiding all major roads and towns. It went through Wingrave, Aston Abbots, Cublington, Whitchurch, Oving, Pitchcott, Upper Winchendon and Chilton.

Leatherslade Farm, near Brill, the remote hiding place of the Great Train Robbers in 1963.

The Gang Assembles

By Tuesday August 6th 1963 the gang began assembling at the farm, including one German man who would make sure that the German backers got their two million pounds pay-off. The robbery was to take place on Thursday, August 13th.

Half a mile north of Bridge No. 127 there were signals on a gantry spanning the track. A further 1,300 yards north, nearer Linslade, there were also dwarf signals at trackside. Both gantry and dwarf signals were far from any dwelling.

The plan was basically simple – to obscure the signal on the gantry by stuffing a heavy gauntlet glove in front of it, and substituting alongside a rogue signal lamp worked from a battery. All telephone wires would be cut. At the right moment the green signals would disappear and red signals would take their place. This would halt the train. When that happened, several actions would be carried out simultaneously. Each man knew what he had to do.

The locomotive and the front two coaches would be uncoupled from the rest of the train; the guard would be overpowered; the engine driver would be replaced by another driver – a retired railwayman who had been recruited by the gang. The locomotive and the front two coaches, including the all-important HVP coach, would then be driven the two thousand plus yards to Bridego Bridge. There the vehicles would be waiting in the lane below the bridge. By then, of course, the coaches would have been broken into and the PO workers overpowered.

It didn't quite work out as planned. The retired engine driver couldn't get the engine started! He was ruthlessly pushed to one side, and the mail train's own driver was violently persuaded to drive the engine and the two coaches as far as the bridge. There, working frantically, the gang removed the heavy mail bags out of the coach, onto the track, and from there down the embankment into the lane and onto the vehicles. In their haste they failed to remove all the bags from the coach – only one hundred and twenty bags out of the two hundred and fifty aboard the train were actually taken, and one of these was inadvertently left on the embankment.

The leaders of the gang had decided beforehand how long they could allow themselves for the operation. They decided it was time to get going even though not all the bags had been snatched. So through the country lanes the convoy made its was back safely to Leatherslade Farm. They had their radios tuned in to the frequency used by the Buckinghamshire Police and listened anxiously for their reaction.

When they left the scene of the crime they left the Post

Office workers, the guard and the engine driver tied up on the floor of the train. They yelled at them as they left: 'Stay where you are and do nothing for half an hour or we'll be back!'

That threat later prompted a Buckinghamshire Police Officer to conclude that the robbers would probably go to ground somewhere within a thirty mile radius of Bridego Bridge. Scotland Yard, who had been called in, agreed, and the search was on.

Back at the farm the money counting started. It fell far short of the five million pounds hoped for. The total was in fact £2,600,000. The German representative was told firmly that the German cut must be reduced from two to one million, and with this he had to agree. Even so, what happened that August night just south of Leighton Buzzard was the largest robbery ever to have taken place in this country. And North Buckinghamshire place names became familiar to newspaper readers all over the world.

When the counting and the sharing out was completed the members of the gang abandoned their intention to stay hidden at Leatherslade Farm till Sunday. They were impatient now to be gone. So they scattered, in various vehicles and in various directions. And, as the world now knows, they met various fates.

One after another they were arrested and were brought to their sensational trial in Aylesbury, a trial that lasted more than a month. What happened to them all subsequently is a story as sensational as the story of the robbery itself.

And perhaps the most ironic twist in the story is the fact that part of the evidence that convicted them was the discovery of finger prints on the Monopoly set left at Leatherslade Farm!

Stop Press

In late 1992 planning permission was given to the present owner of Leatherslade Farm to demolish it and build a new house on the site.

Chapter 15

ANCIENT AND MODERN

Cavity wall insulation and recycling are very much 20th century activities. But are they so modern after all? Take Berkhamsted Castle for example!

It was one of nearly five hundred castles ordered by William the Conqueror in the twenty years immediately following his victory in 1066. William's half-brother, Robert of Mortaine, built it. Berkhamsted was built as a 'motte and bailey' castle, meaning that a central motte or mound, crowned by a tower, was surrounded by an outer wall. Within the wall was the 'bailey' comprising various buildings – stores, quarters for retainers, and perhaps a chapel. If the bailey buildings should be overrun the defenders could retreat to the tower on the mound for a last stand. All round, outside the wall, ran a ditch or moat.

Today, nearly one thousand years later, enough still remains of Berkhamsted Castle for us to picture how it was when it was new. But in fact what we see of the ruined walls today is only the *filling* which was once packed between the inner and outer stones of the walls, – 11th century cavity wall insulation in fact! And what happened to all the stones from the original walls? They were carried off, over a period of years as the castle fell into disrepair. And they were used for the erection of other buildings elsewhere. Recycled in fact!

Such recycling of valuable building materials has gone on all though the centuries. Some of it is sufficiently documented for us to know with certainty that building 'A' has been constructed from materials salvaged from building 'B'. More often, we only know that a building was dismantled or fell into disrepair, and can only assume that the building materials would certainly not be wasted.

The Roman Villa which once stood near Bradwell is a case in point. It fell into disrepair after the Romans left in the 4th century. Today only the outlines of its foundations remain. We can be virtually certain that people would have helped themselves to the materials of which the villa had been made, and used them elsewhere for other buildings.

It was not only the 20th century practice of recycling that was anticipated centuries before. So also was central heating! When the remains of Bancroft Roman Villa were discovered near Bradwell it was found that beneath the rich mosaics of the floor there were indications of the underfloor heating which serviced two bath suites.

Milton Keynes boasts a magnificent Shopping Precinct and it also has The Bowl, an arena where an audience of fifty thousand can be accommodated. Verulamium, the Roman City we know as St. Albans also had an arena nearly two thousand years ago. Like The Bowl, it could accommodate fifty thousand people, to enjoy the classical plays, pantomimes, and cock-fighting staged there. And nearby there was also a shopping precinct. True, it comprised only two rows of nine shops plus a courtyard.

In 304 AD a pagan Roman soldier stationed at Verulamium gave shelter to a fugitive Christian and was converted by him. His name was Alban. For his part in helping the fugitive he was taken prisoner and beheaded on a nearby hilltop, becoming the first English martyr. A church was later built on the site of his martyrdom. In the 8th century King Offa II of Mercia founded an Abbey and placed Alban's bones in a special tomb there which became a shrine.

Three hundred years later, after the Norman Conquest, the building of the present Abbey began. This involved a marvellous example of recycling, because considerable quantities of bricks and stones were brought from the ruins of the old Roman City and used in the construction of the new

Abbey church. They can still be seen today, especially in the tower.

Consider next the Chantry Chapel of St. Margaret and St. Catherine which once stood on the Watling Street at Fenny Stratford. We first hear of it as the 'Veny Stratford Capella' in 1460. It was evidently a fairly substantial building, comprising nave, chancel and north aisle together with a tower and four bells. It assumed greater importance in 1494 when a Religious Guild was formed next to the Chapel. Part of the Guild's building still remains, behind the Bull Inn. The Guild used the Chapel for its worship and it provided two priests in its membership to serve the local congregation.

But then came 1547 when all Chantry Chapels and Guilds were abolished all over the country. The Chapel in Fenny was disposed of for what it would fetch in 1551. 'Certain sons of Belial' bought it for £1,572-15-9. They tore it down and carried off the building material for recycling elsewhere. And that, as far as Fenny was concerned, was that. For the next hundred and sixty years Fenny had no place of worship. But then in the 18th century Browne WIllis, the Lord of the Manor, achieved his own form of recycling – he bought the site of the old Chantry Chapel and on it built St. Martin's Church.

Meanwhile, a few miles away at Mursley another great building was coming to grief. It was Salden Manor, the seat of the Fortescue family. Sir John Fortescue, cousin of Elizabeth I, was MP for Buckinghamshire. He built himself a magnificent mansion at Salden near Mursley and often entertained Elizabeth I there. He rose to be Chancellor of the Exchequer. But later the Fortescue family fortunes waned and the great Mansion fell into disrepair. Finally, in 1739, the building was pulled down. Browne Willis made sure that something should be salvaged. For the modest sum of thirty shillings he bought some of the stained glass windows for which Salden had been famous, and he 'recycled' some of these in his own house at Whaddon Hall. Other parts of the stained glass he used in a window for the new church of St. Martin in Fenny Stratford. It is the window in the north-west corner. In the bottom

This window in St. Martin's Church, Fenny Stratford, is made of recycled glass that Browne Willis bought for 30/- when Salden Manor was demolished in 1739. The bottom right hand corner shows the Arms of Anne Boleyn.

right-hand corner of the window can be seen the Fortescue Arms, and the name Anne Boleyn, the executed wife of Henry VIII.

On another occasion Browne Willis was guilty of a cynical piece of recycling. He abominated nonconformity. When a nonconformist chapel was opened in Fenny he took immediate action. He promptly bought the chapel 'to prevent the growth of fanaticism'. He pulled the chapel down and cynically carted off the building materials to recycle them in the new stables he was building at Whaddon Hall.

Domestically Browne Willis was caught up in a long-lasting recycling process concerning his own dwelling. Water Hall had been for centuries the seat of the de Grey family as Lords of the Manors of Water Eaton and Bletchley. It stood between Water Eaton and the Watling Street. Meanwhile in Whaddon there had been the seat of the Giffard family. When the de Grey family acquired the Manor of Whaddon, Lord Grey decided that he preferred Whaddon to Saffron as the place to live. So he pulled down Water Hall and carried off all the building materials to recycle them in a rebuilt Whaddon Hall. It took scores of wagons to carry all the materials. So an enlarged Whaddon Hall arose and Elizabeth I was several times entertained there.

In the 17th century the Manors of Water Eaton, Bletchley and Fenny Stratford passed to the Villiers family, Dukes of Buckingham. But in 1674 Thomas Willis purchased the Manors, and from him they passed, first to his son, and then to his grandson, Browne Willis. By that time work had already started on yet another rebuilding of Whaddon Hall. When Browne Willis came into his inheritance he was faced with many problems. He spent a fortune rebuilding Whaddon Hall, but to little purpose. After his death the new version had to be pulled down and nothing now remains of it. It was the end of a complicated story which had begun centuries before. Not all recycling processes run smoothly.

A final example of recycling. If you visit the Swan Hotel in Bedford you can ascend to the first floor up a magnificent staircase. At its foot an inscription on the wall tells its origin:

THE SWAN HOTEL

This Hotel was built in 1794 by Francis Vth Duke of Bedford to replace the Mediaeval Swan Inn then demolished – in whose Upper Room Elizabeth Bunyan pleaded with the Chief Justice Sir Matthew Hale and Judge Twisden – the Judges on circuit in 1661 – for her husband's liberty. This stairway was installed here by the Duke, having been conveyed from Houghton House (now Houghton Ruins) when dismantled in 1794.

HOUGHTON HOUSE
built in 1616, was once the home of the beautiful Mary Herbert Countess of Pembroke, Sir Philip Sidney's sister . . . Houghton House has been named by long tradition as the original of Bunyan's 'House Beautiful' of the Pilgrim's Progress.

VISITOR!
As you tread this Stairway you pass where the feet of England's great and fair once trod.

❖ ❖ ❖ ❖ ❖

Neighbourhood Watch schemes for the discouragement of crime are a feature of late 20th century life. But they have their predecessors too. On 5th January, 1838, a Public Meeting was convened of:

WINSLOW
ASSOCIATION
for the
PROSECUTION OF THIEVES
It took place at The Bell Inn in Winslow, and it decided to open its membership to 'persons residing or occupying property within the several parishes of Great Horwood, Little Horwood, Swanbourne, Grandborough, East Claydon and Addington'.

So what's ancient, and what's modern?
Perhaps the Book Ecclesiastes in the Bible puts it best:

'The thing that hath been, it is that which shall be; and that which is done is that which shall be done' and there is no new thing under the sun.'

Chapter 16

OPEN UNIVERSITY

You cannot get much for ten pence nowadays. But in the mid-seventies the Open University acquired a church building on a one hundred year lease for ten pence a year! The Church is St. Michael's, Walton. It dates from about 1350 but is on the site of previous church buildings going back to at least 1189.

The Open University was fast developing its campus around Walton Hall. In a shrewd move the OU negotiated the

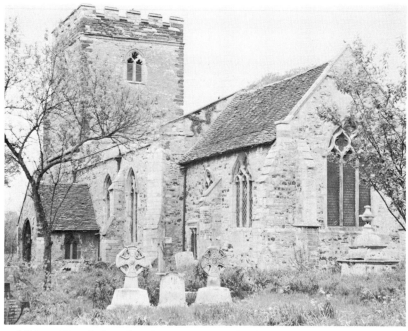

Walton Church, leased to the Open University for 100 years for 10p a year.

OPEN UNIVERSITY

hundred-year lease of St. Michael's Church, a decision pleasing both to the Open University and to the ecclesiastical authorities. The church, which had been declared redundant in 1974, was in a parlous condition. The Open University commissioned architects and contractors to carry out a complete and thorough restoration. This work, which cost £90,000, was completed by 1978. The result is a building in magnificent condition which is in regular use for a variety of functions – social, musical, and educational. The church is also used regularly for worship, as a meeting place for Christian Forum, the interdenominational group based on the OU campus.

Walton was always a very small village. There was no mention of it in the Domesday Survey of 1086. But it is known that a church existed in 1189. Walton had both a Manor and a Hall. Both of these presented priests to the living, apparently in competition! But in 1458 agreement was reached that they would appoint alternately. By the 17th century the two Manors were united. This was achieved by the Gilpin family (one of whose members was the John Gilpin, *'a citizen of credit and renown . . . of famous London town'*, immortalised in William Cowper's long and diverting ballad published in 1785).

In World War II Walton Hall housed forty WRNS who worked at Bletchley Park, the secret Communications establishment which cracked the Nazi Enigma code and cipher machines.

From 1965 to 1968 Walton Hall was empty. In 1968 the new Milton Keynes Development Corporation acquired it and made it their Architects and Planning Office. But they soon moved from Walton Hall to Wavendon Tower. So, by the summer of 1969 Walton Hall stood empty and waiting – waiting for the exciting new chapter about to begin. The Open University officially took possession on 1st September 1969. And on 18th May 1970 the Earl Mountbatten of Burma unveiled the University's Foundation Stone next to the portico of Walton Hall.

The Open University had been given its Royal Charter in May 1969. It was a brave new venture and it was appropriate

129

that it found a home in the new city of Milton Keynes.

But the idea had taken a long time to come to fruition. As early as 1924 it had been suggested that radio could be used in connection with university-level education. The Radio Times of June 1924 contained an article entitled: 'A Broadcasting University'. But nothing came of it. After World War II television began in earnest, and again there were some who foresaw that this exciting new medium could be harnessed to university-level education. But still nothing happened. Meanwhile other countries overseas saw the same possibility, and a start was made in America, Canada, Australia and the Soviet Union, to develop what was called 'distance learning'.

Here in Britain it was Harold Wilson who first propounded the idea of what he called 'A University of the Air'. He made a speech on the subject in Glasgow in 1963. But even then nothing was done to follow up the idea. The official Labour Party did not include it in its policy and it remained only a personal enthusiasm of Harold Wilson.

In 1964 he became Prime Minister. Soon afterwards he charged Jenny Lee, his Minister for the Arts, to get on with the job of turning the idea into a reality. Things moved really fast after that. The site was found, buildings started, and the first staff recruited. The OU was up and running, and in 1971 the first 24,000 students were admitted.

'Distance learning' means that students learn in their own homes. Every course is designed for students studying on their own. They purchase the necessary books and they are helped by radio and TV programmes, and by audio and video tapes. No entry qualifications are needed for any OU courses other than higher degrees. Scattered all over the country are some two hundred and fifty OU Study Centres where students can find help reasonably near their homes. Every student must also attend at least one residential summer school, lasting a week, usually held on the campuses of other Universities around the country during vacations.

The OU offers courses in six faculties – Arts, Social Sciences, Education, Mathematics, Science and Technology. The largest single group of OU students (75,000 in 1991) are working for their BA degree. To complete a BA degree a student needs to complete six credits. Each credit will need some twelve to fourteen hours study each week for nine months of the year. A student can take as long as he likes to accumulate his tally of six credits.

What does it cost the students? They pay tuition fees (currently £218) plus the cost of the residential school (currently £143). They also pay for their books and travel costs. So the minimum cost for the first year's study is likely to approach £400. Assuming a student takes up to five or six years to complete his six credits for his BA degree the total cost to him will have come to about £2,300.

In two short decades the OU has become Britain's largest single teaching institution. More than one hundred thousand students register each year, and over 108,000 have already successfully graduated. About 80% of undergraduates successfully complete their first year examinations. More than 55% go on successfully to graduate between four and six years later. Currently of every one hundred new graduates annually from British universities, eight will have come from the OU. From 1992 enrolment for study with the OU has been made available to students in all the EEC countries.

Harold Wilson has gone on record to say:

'The Open University is my proudest achievement.
I am extremely proud of the fact that as Prime
Minister I was able to initiate the project and to see
it brought to fulfilment during the years of Labour
Government in the sixties'.

Universities are sometimes thought of as either 'ancient' or 'old' or 'redbrick'. As well as being appropriately sited in the new city of Milton Keynes, the OU stands midway between the ancient Universities of Oxford and Cambridge, and about the same distance from the old University of London.

As the waters of the Isis flow through Oxford, the Cam flows through Cambridge, and the Thames through London, so now on the banks of the modest little Ouzel there stands today on its

The Open University. Harold Wilson called it 'my proudest achievement'.

seventy-acre campus the largest educational institution in Britain.

In his 'Portrait of Buckinghamshire' John Camp asked: 'Whether the little hamlet of Walton will retain its identity in the future development of Milton Keynes is problematical. Perhaps it will soon become a memory and vanish with the few memories that still linger in this pleasant countryside of chestnut and red hawthorn'.

He needn't have worried!

Chapter 17

MK MOSAIC

A mosaic is made of so many bits, each one alone insignificant, but put them together in the right way and the result can be truly magnificent.

Mosaic from Bradwell on wall of Shopping Centre, Milton Keynes.

The same is true when you consider a town, take Milton Keynes for example,
It's not just a single dot on the map, it's nothing nearly
so simple.

It's a mosaic whose every part is worth a separate mention.
It's the many parts that make the whole, each deserving
your attention.

There's LAVENDON and WAVENDON, of WOOLSTONES
there are three,
there's WOUGHTON and there's BROUGHTON, and there's
LOUGHTON too you see.
There's FISHERMEAD and LINFORD, and there's
'WILLEN-by-the sea',
and MOUNT FARM also has a lake, and TONGWELL – that
makes three.

There's BRADWELL NEW and BRADWELL OLD, which used
to have an abbey,
too bad that what remains today is altogether shabby.
But its windmill still survives today and stands for all
to see.
And not far off from that same mill are Roman remains
to see.

Of STRATFORDS we can boast a pair, joined by a Roman
road.
FENNY and STONY are the STRATFORDS I mean,
with their Roman WATLING STREET between.

There's COFFEE HALL and OLDBROOK, TINKER'S BRIDGE
and EATON MILL,
and we also have a HEELANDS even if we lack a hill.
COTTENHAM STREAM runs into the OUZEL, and so does the
LOUGHTON BROOK,
and all of them feed the Bedford OUSE, no matter what
course they took.
And making its way across the town there's another
waterway,
complete with many a bridge and lock, giving cruiser
and barge a shorter way.

And finally we have something special
to add to our diversity:
there is no other place but this
can boast an OPEN UNIVERSITY.

SO HERE'S TO ALL THE BITS THAT GO
TO MAKE UP THIS FAIR CITY,
AND HERE'S TO US WHO LIVE IN IT,
WE'RE REALLY SITTING PRETTY.

Chapter 18

CARRYING A TORCH FOR THE LADY WITH THE LAMP

In a speech on October 1st 1939 Churchill said: 'I cannot forecast to you the action of Russia. It is a riddle wrapped in a mystery inside an enigma'.

The same might be said of the life of Florence Nightingale. Everyone knows the story of the great heroine, 'the Lady with the Lamp', of Crimea War fame. Countless biographies and articles have been written about her life and work. Her elder sister, Parthenope, married Sir Harry Verney of Claydon House and Florence frequently stayed in that house, often for long periods. In Claydon House are the two Florence Nightingate rooms, still furnished much as she left them. They are full of memorabilia of the great heroine, evocative not only of the great work she did at Scutari in the Crimea, but also of all her other interests in a long life of public service. She died at the age of ninety in 1910.

Where, then, is the riddle, or the mystery, or the enigma? They are to be found in the fact that in all that has been written about Florence Nightingale, only one obscure publication mentions the fact that at the age of seventeen Florence fell in love with her first cousin, John Smithurst, and he with her. John was thirteen years older than Florence. Because they were first cousins their families forbade the marriage. Out of filial piety and obedience they both accepted the ban. Both vowed to spend their lives serving humanity. Florence went on to find a vocation in nursing, and John was ordained and went as a missionary to Canada. And it was in Canada that that obscure publication appeared. It was entitled 'Elora' and was published in 1930, written by John R Connon. Elora is today a small town of some six thousand inhabitants. In the middle of last century it was little more than a village. It's Anglican church is St. John the Evangelist's and John Smithurst was its Rector for six years starting on New Year's Day, 1852.

Florence's parents, William and Fanny Nightingale, were wealthy, with estates both in Hampshire and Derbyshire. Both were clever, amiable dilettante, fluent in Italian, French, Latin and Greek. William taught both his daughters himself. The family name had not always been Nightingale. Until 1815 it had been Shore, but in that year a sudden accession of wealth caused them to change the name to Nightingale.

The family travelled much abroad and Florence was born on May 12th 1820 in the Italian city of that name. Her elder sister had also been born in Italy and she too had been named after the place of her birth, Parthenope. Some might think this an odd choice of name – the original Parthenope was the Siren who threw herself into the sea out of love for Ulyses!

The Nightingale family knew the best of English intelligentsia, and many foreign literary and social figures as well. William and Fanny were determined that both their daughters should make 'good' marriages. In Parthenope's case they succeeded – she married Sir Harry Verney of Claydon House in North Buckinghamshire. For nine years in the 1840s Monckton Milnes, later Lord Houghton, courted Florence assiduously, much encouraged by Mr and Mrs Nightingale but Florence repeatedly rejected his proposals.

In the meantime, as John Connon tells the story in 'Elora', Florence had met her first cousin John Smithurst, and they had fallen in love. This was the last thing her parents wanted. To complicate things still further, there was a third cousin, William Shore, who also fell in love with Florence! That engagement too was sternly forbidden. Crestfallen, William Shore emigrated to the United States. The 'evidence' for this twist to the story is a news item in a Wisconsin paper in 1910. It read:

'FOX LAKE, WIS., AUGUST 18 – The death of Florence Nightingale, 'The Angel of the Crimea', in London this week, recalls a very pretty romance, in which Fox Lake is indirectly interested. William Shore and Florence Nightingale were cousins and lovers in England in the long ago. English law forbids the marriage of cousins, so they pledged their troth and separated, neither ever to marry. William Shore drifted to Fox Lake, and lived here many years, finally dying in 1868, and his remains are now resting in beautiful Waushara Cemetery in this village. Florence Nightingale remained faithful to her vow'.

So if this story be true, John Smithurst in his love for Florence had a rival in his other cousin, William Shore. In the event this didn't matter because that parental ban meant that neither cousin could marry Florence. As Connon tells the story, both Florence and John, reluctantly accepting that they could not marry, agreed to part. Both resolved to pursue vocations in which they could sublimate their disappointment in work for others.

In John's case this meant ordination and missionary work. He went to the Training College of The Church Missionary Society (CMS) in Islington and in 1839 he was ordained by the Bishop of London. In that same year CMS sent him to Canada. There, at Red River Settlement in Hudson Bay Territory he was appointed Chaplain to the Company, with official accommodation at Fort Garry (now Winnipeg in Manitoba). But John was more interested in working with and for the Red Indians and soon asked to be released from his Chaplain's duties. He moved into the Indian village and spent the next twelve years working there. His labours were by no means confined to the conventional work of a priest. He became a farmer too, and taught his flock how to cope with the problems of the hard winters by laying up supplies of grain and meat in the summer months to see them through the winter. He started schools and, having learned the Cree language, he published books.

After twelve years of such arduous work he returned to England in 1851. He stayed almost a year in England, hoping that after all he might be allowed to marry Florence. But that was not to be. So he returned to Canada, this time to Ontario. On January 1st 1852 he began work as the Rector of St. John's Church in Elora, an incumbency that lasted six years.

It is perhaps no coincidence that the year 1851 which John spent in England was the very year when Florence at last began her work as a nurse. John had therefore to accept that not only was marriage to her ruled out by parental opposition, but it was also precluded by Florence's own immersion in her chosen vocation in nursing. Whatever the future might hold for Florence, there would be no role for her as a missionary's wife in Canada.

One can imagine how they must have talked these matters out in 1851. John, disappointed, returned to Canada. And perhaps one can see at this point the significance of the greatest treasure the Church in Elora possesses. This comprises a complete set of silver Communion vessels – Chalice, Paten and Wine Flagon. These are inscribed as having been a gift to John. The inscription is in Latin and its wording is very odd. It runs:

DONO DEDIT HOC MUNUSCULUM REVERENDO JOANNO SMITHURST AMICO DELICTISSIMO ALUMNUS EJUS EBENEZER HALL OFFICIORUM IN SE GRATE MEMOR. AD MDCCCLII

Translated freely into English this becomes:

ACTING AS AGENT FOR SOMEONE EBENEZER HALL GAVE AS A GIFT THIS SET OF COMMUNION SILVER TO THE REVEREND JOHN SMITHURST, A VERY DEAR FRIEND, IN GRATEFUL RECOGNITION OF HIS MANY KINDNESSES. AD 1852.

Now that is surely a very odd way to commemorate a gift. It can only mean that for some reason the donor did not want the name of the giver made public, and so used an agent to convey the gift. They have no doubt in Elora that the donor was Florence Nightingale. Notice the date of the gift – 1852 – the very year after John's lonely return to Canada.

John bequeathed that silver Communion set to the Elora church and it is there, behind plate glass, to this day. Below it is a card on which is boldly printed the 'fact' that the Communion silverware was a gift to John from Florence.

There is a very recent postscript to this part of the tale. In 1991 a young man from the nearby town of Kitchener broke into the church and stole the Communion vessels. The Police suggested that perhaps some publicity on TV might help to solve the crime. Accordingly, interviews were conducted in the press and on TV with the present Rector. These stressed the unique and historic significance of the Communion silverware. This evidently frightened the life out of the young thief who couldn't get rid of his ill-gotten loot fast enough. He dumped it all in a rubbish skip from which, happily, it was recovered. The items are now once more safely behind plate glass in Elora Church.

Also in the church are two stained-glass windows side by side on the south wall, one to John Smithurst, Rector, and the other to Florence, 'The Lady with the Lamp'.

Nor is that all. For the past ten years Elora has had an annual Festival. It lasts for two weeks and the programme encompasses a wide range of musical and other entertainment. The highlight of the 1992 Festival was the WORLD PREMIÈRE no less, of a new Chamber Opera entitled 'Florence, The Lady with the Lamp'. In operatic form it tells the love story of Florence Nightingale and John Smithurst. Four nights of the Festival were given over to the Opera.

There is no question then – in Elora they are convinced that their one-time Rector had been in love with Florence Nightingale long before she achieved international fame as the heroine of the Crimea.

They have much local folklore to support the story. And they have one piece of written 'evidence' too. John Smithurst died in 1867 and is buried in Elora Cemetery. In his last illness he was treated by a young Dr Paget. Dr Paget practised in Elora for sixty years. Then he retired and lived on to a great age in Toronto. In 1910 when news of the death of Florence Nightingale was received in Canada, old Dr Paget was asked about this oft-repeated tale of the Nightingale/Smithurst romance. In reply Dr Paget wrote this brief but forthright letter:

Jarvis Street,
Toronto,
August 17th 1910

'I had the pleasure of knowing the late Reverend John Smithurst of Lea Hurst, Minto; a fine educated gentleman. He was engaged to the late Florence Nightingale. I attended him, with Dr Clarke of Guelph, during his last illness'.

The mystery remains, then. How is it that this romance, so confidently believed in at Elora, finds no mention in any of the unnumerable biographies of Florence, or in any of the hundreds of articles about her that have appeared over the years? Specifically, how is it that nowhere in the thousand pages of Sir Edward Cook's monumental two-volume biography of Florence Nightingale is there a single reference to John Smithurst? And how is it that no mention, or even hint of that long-ago romance can be found in any of the thousands of documents and letters which Florence left behind?

Perhaps the answer, or part of it, lies in Florence's nature and character. It takes nothing away from the splendid service she rendered in the Crimea and afterwards, to point out what a tyrranical person she could be. She could be ruthless, obstinate, obsessional, and fiercely critical. She achieved all that she did precisely because she was all of these things. In an age when nurses were thought of as socially beyond the pale – as untrained, coarse and uncouth, and often as drunks and prostitutes, she determined to take up nursing and to make that

$1.00

The Love Story
of
Florence Nightingale
and
John Smithurst

The Church of St. John the Evangelist
Elora, Ontario

Did the Rector once carry a torch for the Lady with the Lamp?

profession both honourable and respectable. To achieve her objective she had to fight her own family and society at large. And she succeeded.

That successful struggle marked her out as a redoubtable fighter in an age when society neither expected nor wanted a woman to achieve such dominance. It would not easily have marked her out as the future wife of an obscure missionary in faraway Canada.

It could well be too that even if, momentarily at seventeen, she had affection for her cousin John, he never loomed as large on her horizon as she undoubtedly did on his.

If, instead of going on to fame in the Crimea she had instead gone on to be the wife of the Rector of Elora in Ontario, there might still be the Florence Nightingale rooms in Claydon House but their contents would be totally different.

In Elora Church, for a dollar, you can buy a ten-page booklet entitled 'The Love Story of Florence Nightingale and John Smithurst'. With fine hyperbole the pamphlet ends with the ringing challenge:

It may well be that as the facts become better known, the love story of Florence Nightingale and John Smithurst will take rank as one of the greatest love stories of history. Whatever the world may say, Canadians at least will not forget John Smithurst whose story is here made public for the first time'.

Meanwhile, for the rest of the world perhaps, the story remains 'a riddle wrapped in a mystery inside an enigma', while Ontarians in Elora continue to honour John Smithurst, the priest who carried a torch for The Lady with the Lamp.

Chapter 19

RANDOM ROUNDABOUT

Finally, here are some facts you might not know about.

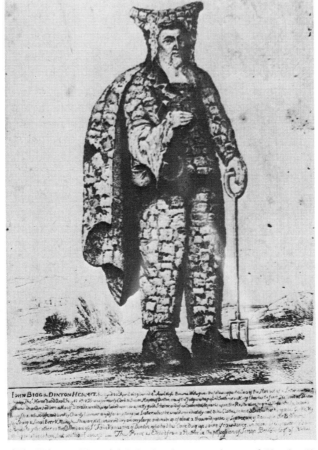

'The Dinton Hermit'. Was he the executioner of Charles I?

Do you know why the pub in the village of Ford is called 'The Dinton Hermit'? Who was that hermit? He was a very learned man named John Bigg. In the 17th century he was Secretary to Simon Mayne of Dinton Hall. Simon Mayne was one of the twenty-six men who signed the death warrant of King Charles I. When the Civil War ended, Oliver Cromwell ruled England as Protector for eleven years. But in 1660 the monarchy was restored and King Charles II came to the throne of his late father. As many as possible of the regicides were arrested and put on trial. One of them was Simon Mayne. He escaped execution but only because he died while a prisoner in the Tower of London.

All this was too much for his faithful Secretary, John Bigg, whose mind became unhinged. For years afterwards he lived in the hedgerows as a hermit, begging for food. He became famous for his extraordinary shoes which he kept for years, patching and repatching them by adding fresh strips of leather

The Pub at Ford is named after him.

year after year. One of his shoes is in the Ashmolean Museum in Oxford. It was alleged by some that John Bigg had been the executioner of King Charles I. The pub at Ford, a tiny village two miles from Dinton, is called The Dinton Hermit. Gone, but not forgotten.

Very near to Dinton is the tiny hamlet of Gibralter. Its improbable name derives from the fact that it stands on a great slab of rock. Twice in times past tragedy struck the little community at Gibralter. In 1665, when the Great Plague was raging in London, a sizeable group of Londoners walked all the way from the capital to Gibralter to escape the plague. One of the group had a relative in the village. Unfortunately one of the group brought the infection with them. As a result there were forty deaths in Gibralter.

THIS
TABLET WAS ERECTED BY
M. LEE
MEDICAL OFFICER OF CUDDINGTON PARISH
TO THE MEMORY OF
48 PERSONS RESIDING AT GIBRALTER
WHO WERE CUT OFF IN AUGUST 1849
AFTER A FEW HOURS ILLNESS
BY ASIATIC CHOLERA.

WATCH THEREFORE FOR YE KNOW NOT
WHAT HOUR YOUR LORD DOTH COME.

The tiny village of Gibralter, near Dinton, lost half its population to cholera in 1849. Earlier, in 1665, forty villagers had died in the Great Plague.

In 1849 history repeated itself. There was a cholera epidemic in many parts of England, and Gibralter did not escape. As the number of cases increased the villagers of Gibralter fled their houses and camped in the open. A tablet was later erected on Cuddington Churchyard wall 'to the memory of forty-eight persons, residents of Gibralter, who were cut off in August 1849 after a few hours' illness by Asiatic Cholera'.

When Henry VIII renounced the supremacy of the Pope over the English Church, he ordered that all the old Catholic Prayerbooks should be destroyed. This was too much for Thomas Andrews, the Parish Priest of Addington. So he hid his precious books by walling them up in the north wall of the chancel of his church. He also hid a small 'Super Altar', a 14th century slate slab on which the sacred vessels were placed on the Altar at Mass. The six books, and the 'Super Altar' remained hidden for nearly three hundred years. They came to light by accident in 1857 when part of the church was being rebuilt. The slate slab was let into the altar of Addington church when the restoration was carried out.

The County Hall in Aylesbury was completed in 1740. Many a notable trial took place there up to 1970 when Assizes and Quarter Sessions ceased there. Up to 1845 it was also the scene of many public executions. The 'drop' was installed on the main balcony, so that the assembled public could both see and hear the condemed.

One of these was a young man named Constable. His mother kept The King's Head in Stony Stratford. Young Constable had been arrested for sheep-stealing. He was found guilty and hanged at Aylesbury. His mother brought his body back to Stony Stratford for burial. But before the interrment she put the body on show at Stony Fair, charging a penny a peep!

In 1970 the County Hall was gutted by fire. With commendable haste it was fully restored within twelve months. Great care was taken with detail in the reconstruction, including the retention of the secret cupboard behind the Judge's seat. In that cupboard there is a large china chamber pot emblazoned with the County Coat of Arms.

North Bucks. is fortunate in possessing three examples of the work of Grinling Gibbons, the celebrated sculptor. He was famous for his woodcarving, but he also worked in marble. Soulbury Church has an example of his work in both mediums. It is a memorial to the Lovett family, comprising an urn with cherubs, carved in marble, surmounted by a woodcarving of a black wolf. A member of the Lovett family had been Master of Wolfhounds to William the Conqueror. The third local example of Grinling Gibbons' work is the exquisite Font cover in Willen Church.

It is a feature of the Channel Tunnel that road vehicles have to be driven onto the trains for conveyance to and from France. That is not such a new idea. A hundred and fifty years ago, when the railway was being laid between London and Birmingham, there was a period of several months when there was a gap in the line between Bletchley and Rugby, waiting for the completion of the Kilsby Tunnel. During that period Birmingham coaches from London were loaded onto flat-cars at Euston and carried as far as Denbigh. They were there unloaded and carried their passengers on to Rugby by road. In 1920 Sir Herbert and Lady Leon unveiled a plaque commemorating this fact on the south side of Denbigh Bridge.

Mention of the Leons prompts thoughts of Bletchley Park, their mansion which the Government bought just before World War II for a Communications Centre. It achieved world-wide fame as the home of 'Enigma' and the cracking of Germany's secret cipher machines. Less well-known is the fact that in World War II the exiled Czech Government set up its Headquarters in Britain in this area, when Czechoslovakia had been overrun by the Nazis. Their Headquarters were at Wingrave Manor, a rambling Victorian Mansion later known as Mount Tabor.

Wingrave Manor was the Headquarters of the exiled Czech Government in World War II.

❖ ❖ ❖ ❖ ❖

There are two Winchendons, Upper and Lower. Upper Winchendon has a little Norman Church dedicated to St. Mary Magdalene. It has a very fine 15th century pulpit unique because it is carved from a solid block of wood. It was from this pulpit that John Wesley preached his very first sermon, on 3 October, 1725, after his ordination in Oxford.

Nether Winchendon boasts a church clock with one hand.

St. Nicholas Church, Lower Winchendon, goes one better. It has a monumental three-decker pulpit dated 1613. Even more unusual is the church clock, which only has one hand. It began life in the Manor House and was moved to the church in 1722. Its pendulum, fourteen feet long, can be seen swinging at the base of the tower every 1.89 seconds. The 18th century clock is one of only half a dozen of this type in this country, and it maintains a high degree of accuracy.

On the green outside Lower Winchendon Church there is a curious Victorian letterbox, set in a stone pillar with a ball on top.

❖ ❖ ❖ ❖ ❖

*The fine Jacobean
three-decker pulpit, in
Nether Winchendon
Church.*

*Nether Winchendon's
splendid Victorian Pillar
Box.*

151

On the Vestry wall of St. James Church, Great Horwood, there are photographs of a number of former incumbents. One of them was John Chevallier. He was Rector of Great Horwood from 1889 to 1917. Beneath his portrait are inscribed a number of biographical details, concluding with the words: 'During the German War he taught Mathematics at Giggleswick School, Yorkshire, and was accidentally killed by a cyclist using lights obscured against aircraft' – an interesting little footnote to history.

❖ ❖ ❖ ❖ ❖

TO THE BELOVED MEMORY OF
CAPTAIN THE RIGHT HON.
NEIL JAMES
ARCHIBALD PRIMROSE
M.P. FOR WISBECH AND M.C.
BORN AT DALMENY DEC.14.1882
AND KILLED NOV. 15.1917
WHILE LEADING A CHARGE
OF THE ROYAL BUCKS HUSSARS
AT THE HILL OF GEZER
NEAR WHICH AT RAMLEH
HE LIES BURIED
THIS TABLET IS ERECTED BY HIS
PROUD AND SORROWFUL FATHER

NOW HE IS DEAD
FAR HENCE HE LIES
IN THE LORN SYRIAN TOWN
AND ON HIS GRAVE
WITH SHINING EYES
THE SYRIAN STARS LOOK DOWN

Lord Rosebery's brother was killed leading the Royal Bucks. Hussars in the last Calvary Charge made by the British Army – in 1917 at El Mughar in Palestine. His Memorial is in Mentmore Church.

Mentmore Church has a memorial to Neil James Primrose, brother of Lord Rosebery. He was killed leading a Charge by the Royal Bucks Hussars in Palestine in November, 1917, at El Mughar. This was the last Cavalry Charge in the history of the British Army.

Mentmore was the seat of Lord Rosebery. It was sold and is now the world headquarters of the Transcendental Meditation Movement. Lord Rosebery was a great Patron of the Turf. Many of his horses won the great classic races. In the grounds of Mentmore many of his famous horses lie buried. In the equine cemetary there used to stand a magnificent statue of King Tom, the stallion which sired many of the great horses buried there, but this has now been moved to Scotland.

Mentmore Towers, once the seat of Lord Rosebery, now the World Headquarters of the Transcendental Meditation Movement, and of the Natural Law Party.

❖ ❖ ❖ ❖ ❖

Near the old Lovett School in Soulbury is a huge boulder. Tradition says it has magic properties and rolled into Soulbury of its own volition! In fact the truth of its origin is hardly less strange. Experts describe it as a 'glacial erratic' originating from Derbyshire and stranded here when the ice retreated.

The Soulbury Boulder, according to some, has magic qualities and rolled into the village of its own volition. The remarkable fact is that it is a 'glacial erratic', originating from Derbyshire, stranded here at the end of the Ice Age.

❖ ❖ ❖ ❖ ❖

Every once in a while there occur sales of Lordship-of-the-Manor titles. There was such a sale in London in December 1990 when thirty such titles came on the market. One of the titles on offer was that of Lord of the Manor of Stony Stratford. The successful purchaser paid £19,000 for it. 'To the Manor Bought', so to speak.

So the new owner of the title of Lord of the Manor of Stony Stratford can now use the title on his Driving Licence, Passport, cheque book and credit cards. But he must make it clear that he is only Lord of the Manor of Stony Stratford. The 'of' makes it clear that his title is in so sense that of a true peer. Good Lord no!

A few miles from Brill lies Leatherslade Farm which became famous as the hide-out used by the Great Train Robbers in 1963. In much the same area lies Spa Farm which in 1830 so nearly became famous as Dorton Spa. A Company was formed in that year to promote the supposed benefits of a spring in the woods. A Prospectus set out in glowing terms the healthful effects to be had from drinking the waters there. A start was made on erecting suitable buildings. Three bands were hired and a Fireworks Display organised. In 1834 a Promenade Concert attracted three hundred visitors. Then came the best news of all – the young Princess Victoria, the future Queen, intimated that she wished to come to sample the waters of Dorton Spa herself. Alas, she changed her mind, and went to Leamington instead. Overnight Dorton Spa collapsed, and Mr Ricketts, its Promoter, had to abandon the scheme. The Vale of Aylesbury was not, after all, to have a Spa to rival Leamington and Buxton.

'Oh, East is East, and West is West,
and never the twain shall meet,
Till Earth and Sky stand presently
at God's great Judgement Seat.'

Is it true, as some say, that Rudyard Kipling was inspired to write these lines while waiting to change trains at Bletchley, on a journey between Oxford and Cambridge?

INDEX

Books Published by THE BOOK CASTLE

CHANGES IN OUR LANDSCAPE: ASPECTS OF BEDFORDSHIRE, BUCKINGHAMSHIRE and the CHILTERNS, 1947–1992: from the photographic work of Eric Meadows. 350+ fascinating colour and monochrome pictures by the area's leading landscape photographer. Detailed introduction and captions.

JOURNEYS INTO HERTFORDSHIRE: Anthony Mackay. Foreword by The Marquess of Salisbury, Hatfield House. Nearly 200 superbly detailed ink drawings depict the towns, buildings and landscape of this still predominantly rural county.

JOURNEYS INTO BEDFORDSHIRE: Anthony Mackay. Foreword by The Marquess of Tavistock, Woburn Abbey. A lavish book of over 150 evocative ink drawings.

NORTH CHILTERNS CAMERA, 1863–1954: FROM THE THURSTON COLLECTION IN LUTON MUSEUM: edited by Stephen Bunker. Rural landscapes, town views, studio pictures and unique royal portraits by the area's leading early photographer.

LEAFING THROUGH LITERATURE: WRITERS' LIVES IN HERTFORDSHIRE AND BEDFORDSHIRE: David Carroll. Illustrated short biographies of many famous authors and their connections with these counties.

THROUGH VISITORS' EYES: A BEDFORDSHIRE ANTHOLOGY: edited by Simon Houfe. Impressions of the county by famous visitors over the last four centuries, thematically arranged and illustrated with line drawings.

THE HILL OF THE MARTYR: AN ARCHITECTURAL HISTORY OF ST. ALBANS ABBEY: Eileen Roberts. Scholarly and readable chronological narrative history of Hertfordshire and Bedfordshire's famous cathedral. Fully illustrated with photographs and plans.

LOCAL WALKS: SOUTH BEDFORDSHIRE and NORTH CHILTERNS: Vaughan Basham. Twenty-seven thematic circular walks.

CHILTERN WALKS: HERTFORDSHIRE, BEDFORDSHIRE and NORTH BUCKINGHAMSHIRE: Nick Moon. Completes the trilogy of circular walks, in association with the Chiltern Society.

CHILTERN WALKS: BUCKINGHAMSHIRE: Nick Moon. In association with the Chiltern Society, one of a series of three guides to the whole Chilterns. Thirty circular walks.

CHILTERN WALKS: OXFORDSHIRE and WEST BUCKINGHAMSHIRE: Nick Moon. In association with the Chiltern Society, another book of thirty circular walks.

ECHOES: TALES and LEGENDS of BEDFORDHSIRE and HERTFORDSHIRE: Vic Lea. Thirty, compulsively retold historical incidents.

COUNTRY AIR: SUMMER and AUTUMN: Ron Wilson. The Radio Northampton presenter looks month by month at the countryside's wildlife, customs and lore.

COUNTRY AIR: WINTER and SPRING: Ron Wilson. This companion volume completes the year in the countryside.

WHIPSNADE WILD ANIMAL PARK: 'MY AFRICA': Lucy Pendar. Foreword by Andrew Forbes. Introduction by Gerald Durrell. Inside story of sixty years of the Park's animals and people – full of anecdotes, photographs and drawings.

FARM OF MY CHILDHOOD, 1925–1947: Mary Roberts. An almost vanished lifestyle on a remote farm near Flitwick.

SWANS IN MY KITCHEN: The Story of a Swan Sanctuary: Lis Dorer. Foreword by Dr Philip Burton. Tales of her dedication to the survival of these beautiful birds through her sanctuary near Hemel Hempstead.

A LASTING IMPRESSION: Michael Dundrow. An East End boy's wartime experiences as an evacuee on a Chilterns farm at Totternhoe.

EVA'S STORY: CHESHAM SINCE the TURN of the CENTURY: Eva Rance. The ever-changing twentieth-century, especially the early years at her parents' general stores, Tebby's, in the High Street.

DUNSTABLE DECADE: THE EIGHTIES: – A Collection of Photographs: Pat Lovering. A souvenir book of nearly 300 pictures of people and events in the 1980s.

DUNSTABLE IN DETAIL: Nigel Benson. A hundred of the town's buildings and features, plus town trail map.

OLD DUNSTABLE: Bill Twaddle. A new edition of this collection of early photographs.

BOURNE AND BRED: A DUNSTABLE BOYHOOD BETWEEN THE WARS: Colin Bourne. An elegantly written, well-illustrated book capturing the spirit of the town over fifty years ago.

ROYAL HOUGHTON: Pat Lovering. Illustrated history of Houghton Regis from the earliest times to the present.

MURDERS and MYSTERIES, PEOPLE and PLOTS: A Buckinghamshire, Bedfordshire and Northamptonshire Miscellany: John Houghton. This fascinating book of true tales roams around three counties and covers three centuries.

THE CHANGING FACE OF LUTON: An Illustrated History:
Stephen Bunker, Robin Holgate and Marian Nichols. Luton's development from earliest times to the present busy industrial town. Illustrated in colour and monochrome. The three authors from Luton Museum are all experts in local history, archaeology, crafts and social history.

BETWEEN THE HILLS: The Story of Lilley, a Chiltern Village:
Roy Pinnock. A priceless piece of our heritage – the rural beauty remains but the customs and way of life described here have largely disappeared.

THE MEN WHO WORE STRAW HELMETS: POLICING LUTON, 1840–1974: Tom Madigan. Meticulously chronicled history; dozens of rare photographs; author served Luton Police for nearly fifty years.

THE TALL HITCHIN SERGEANT: A Victorian Crime Novel based on fact: Edgar Newman. Mixes real police officers and authentic background with an exciting storyline.

Specially for Children

ADVENTURE ON THE KNOLLS: A STORY OF IRON AGE BRITAIN:
Michael Dundrow. Excitement on Totternhoe Knolls as ten-year-old John finds himself back in those dangerous times, confronting Julius Caesar and his army.

THE RAVENS: ONE BOY AGAINST THE MIGHT OF ROME:
James Dyer. On the Barton hills and in the south-east of England as the men of the great fort of Ravensburgh (near Hexton) confront the invaders.

Further titles are in preparation.
All the above are available via any bookshop, or from the publisher and bookseller

THE BOOK CASTLE
12 Church Street, Dunstable, Bedfordshire, LU5 4RU
Tel: (0582) 605670